Love Song in Harvest

Love-Song in Harvest

An interpretation of
The Book of Ruth

by

GEOFFREY T. BULL

CHRISTIAN LITERATURE CRUSADE

FORT WASHINGTON   PENNSYLVANIA 19034

CHRISTIAN LITERATURE CRUSADE
Fort Washington, Pennsylvania 19034

CANADA
1440 Mackay Street, Montreal, Quebec

This edition 1976 by special arrangement with the British
publisher Pickering & Inglis Ltd.

ISBN 0 87508-042-1

Contents

Preface

In sending forth this interpretation of The Book of Ruth I wish to acknowledge my indebtedness to the spiritual insight and scholarly research of others who have written on this area of Scripture before me. In the Bibliography I mention specially several books of reference.

Whilst local colour and historical background may give some ground for a certain amount of conjecture regarding Ruth's earlier connections, it is anticipated that the discerning reader will distinguish between that which is essentially Biblical and the more imaginative passages of the narrative.

GEOFFREY BULL

Acknowledgements

We would like to thank Hodder & Stoughton Limited, London and William Morrow & Co. Inc., New York for permission to reprint the extract from *The Bible as History* by Werner Keller; Mrs. Frank Houghton for permission to reprint verses of the hymn 'Thou Who wast rich beyond all splendour' by Frank Houghton; and The Psalms & Hymns Trust for permission to reprint a verse of the hymn 'I cannot tell why He, whom angels worship' by William Y. Fullerton.

Indulgence is begged in case of failure to reach any other author or holder of copyrighted portions.

Prologue

'The Spirit of God moved . . .

Gen. 1 : 2

. . . men were moved by the Holy Spirit

2 Pet. 1 : 21

GOD, our Maker, is the Master of Movement. Stillness is relative. Our scientists, who turn the stones and split the atoms, have yet to find a static thing. All is vibrant. There is no matter without motion; no mind, however placid, devoid of current thinking. God is alive and personal, the God of the living. Only death is still; but death is alien. No graves were ever dug in Eden. The Lord God walked there with the man He made. Communion issues in progression. There is no standstill fellowship. God is in-bringing, up-surging, on-going, out-flowing. Who goes with God, goes on!

Space is the 'outspread of His power', the catalyst of Time and Things; the context of 'Our Great Contemporary' and His communication. He fills the universe. What can exclude Him? Who evade? First He is immanent, and then, Emmanuel. He creates and permeates, but then at last, incarnate, comes to earth. He is detached; and yet involved; distant but near; apart yet not apartheid. 'God is not a man that He should lie' but He became man. Though found as we are, He remained what He was. As God omniscient, He knew our structure. As man obedient, He learned our plight. Each creature's movement wakes the sensitivity of God. He is totally cognisant. A reed is shaken in the wind; He notes its bruising. An ant has business? Then He, Himself, will mark its way. The rodent's lair, the locusts' band, the gecko in the house of kings, all speak His vital wisdom in the merest things. The eagle plunging to its prey, the serpent's stealth, the restless sea proclaim the wonder of the God who acts; of Him who feels.[1]

And should my hands reach out to clasp her, His mystery lies in our embrace. God's touch and tenderness are with us, a holiness in love's devotion. Each stir of flesh and spirit reach

9

Him. His gift of nearness cradles life. In Him we move and have our being. God will never be oblivious. 'He knows the way His creatures take'; and 'the way of a man with a maid'.

But should my soul light up with Jesus, then all my heart goes out to meet Him; reason falls silent and the spirit soars. Hence to a yielding in the highest regions and a taste of union yet more sweet. Can ecstasy exceed experience? Oneness with God is the affirmative. His voice is like the sound of waters, whispering, roaring, carolling, calling. He comes my Everlasting Lover, leaping upon the mountains and skipping on the hills. My soul is like a chariot and its prancing horses.[2] But then to the dawn and the quiet of the garden. 'Where art thou?' He asks me. 'Rise up my fair one and come away!'

There is no doubt. God moves! God loves! God feels! He speaks to me. Then whither shall I go but to Emmanuel?

There is no other. My refuge still, is in His everlasting arms.

NOTES

1. See Proverbs 30: 18, 19
2. See Cant. 6: 12

One

Thread of Gold

> '*I will not give sleep to mine eyes, or slumber to mine*
> *eyelids, Until I find out a place for the Lord, an*
> *habitation for the Mighty God of Jacob.*
>
> > '*Lo, we heard of it at Ephratah:*
> > *We found it in the fields . . .*
> > *We will go in . . .*
> > *We will worship at His footstool.*'
> > > Psalm 132: 4–6

ONCE I thought of Naomi, thought of her at Bethlehem, when the years had rolled away . . .

There was a big flat stone in the courtyard and a gnarled, old mulberry. She felt the stone. It was warm to her touch and her hand lingered, almost affectionately. Then she flicked away the sand and sat down. The light was sweet; so bright there on the mountain.

Beyond the gate lay a vista of blue; hills vague and drowsy in the heat, a land of memories. Nor would she go back. She had buried them there. This was the new time. The old time was fading. The God, whom she loved, was wiping her tears.

A breeze stirred faintly in the scented foliage. The leaves waxed talkative. They clapped their hands, then satisfied, kept silence. Two dark, brown eyes, rich as the resin in the snow, shone with eternity. Two little eyelids closed. Long years had passed since fingers so diminutive, had clasped her breast. Her emptiness was filled. Maternally, she pursed her crinkled lips and fondly kissed the infant's cheek. She felt the freshness of the newly born, cool as a petal. She breathed the living calm. The hush and stillness of the highlands, imparted the immensity of God.

And now she worshipped, the love-child resting in her arms. So too, would agéd Simeon, when Obed's line, climaxed at last

in Obed's Lord. She crooned her chosen lullaby, a song of Him,
'who left not off His kindness to the living and the dead'.

From the hamlet of Bethlehem and the fields of Ephratah, the
rock-strewn wadis fell away in dark ravines to the Vale of
Jordan. On sparkling days the fields of Moab stood out greenly
in the gulf below, a world apart . . . That was the way their feet
had taken, she and Elimelech, and their two young boys; the
way down to Moab and the way out from God. The way by
which twelve months ago, she had finally returned.

Her furrowed face still told of tears and scars; her distant
gaze, of other scenes and sons departed. Yet in this sleeping
child the weight of widowhood found recompense. Her tragedy
had now conceived and brought forth destiny. Ruth's firstborn son had made her dead name live. One next of kin, had
kinsman been.

Along the hilltop path, the peasant girls filed by, each poised
in elegance against the azure heaven. Some halted briefly for a
greeting, then glimpsed the young one in the old one's arms.
Glad for a respite in their arduous climb, they shelved their
loads upon the crude stonewall and tiptoed softly to the child.
'A son for Naomi,' they whispered. She shared their wonder.
'He is the restorer of your life,' they chanted, 'your nourisher in
time of age. The one who loves you, bore him for you. Would
seven sons be equal to her?'

Such feminine emotion brought lustre to each work-worn
face. Rough hands reached tenderly to touch the babe. They
longed to hold him, feel his movement; and in that treasured,
fleeting moment, make him their own.

A wisp of mist, like comet's hair, crept through the sunlight.
It turned to gold. The vista of the valleys fled, eclipsed in shade.
Time seemed no more. Ephratah's fields were flushed with
glory. Far out and upward on the dispersed light, the voice of
hosts, unnumbered sang . . . Would not the shepherds from the
defiles hear it? Would not the hills of Judah echo it? This
heavenly song to earth descending, this song of the Child?

The sun went down, proclaimed in blood, throughout the
western sky. The girls took up their loads and sought their
homeward way. Across the shoulders of the hills, low cloud
spread fleece-like, flecked with gold. The day was spent.

Soon must a later day be born; another Child be seen and sung. Obed must grow and bring forth Jesse; of Jesse, David must arise, till in the fullness of God's time, Jesus-Emmanuel be born, of royal David's line . . .

And so I thought of Naomi, thought of her at Bethlehem; looked on 'her son', and leaping through the years, thought on the One, in whom the ultimate restoring lay . . . I came again at sundown, to a courtyard and its stones, where a way led out of splendour, bearing footmarks of the Saviour; where God, Himself, was cradled, just there above Ephratah, in the lowly scent of hay.

Two

Dagger and Trumpet

> '*If I forget . . . let my right hand forget her cunning.*'
> Psalm 137: 5
> '*Now know I that the Lord saveth . . . with the saving strength of His right hand.*'
> Psalm 20: 6

SOME twelve years prior to Obed's birth, there lived in Benjamin, a youth by the name of Ehud.[1] That was at the time of the Moabite oppression, when for eighteen bitter years, Eglon, their obese and ruthless king, ruled over The Land from Jericho, The City of Palm Trees. Since its total destruction in the days of Joshua, no one had dared rebuild the city due to the curse he invoked,[2] though the Kenites, who were descendants of Jethro, had for a while, used its stones to shelter their flocks and had drawn water from its wells. With increasing alien incursions, however, they had retreated to Arad in the hills of southern Judah and the Moabites had attained possession.[3]

Eglon, of course, cared nothing for Jehovah, or the curses on Jericho. To him its ruinous heaps were a strongpoint and a natural pivot for all his strategy in Israel. From his garrison there, he deployed at least ten thousand troops west of Jordan, and in consequence, exerted a stranglehold upon the hill economies of Benjamin and Judah.

Such was the baneful outcome of the spiritual degeneracy and moral decline in Israel. Harassed by the relentless invader and threatened with starvation in the mountains, the elders of Benjamin decided on a policy of appeasement. Their oppressor must be wooed by an impressive gift and negotiations begun, which, though costly, would somehow ensure the survival of their people. This decision had been hard to make and the wrangling bitter, for Benjamin, though least amongst the tribes,

14

was ever proud at heart. Ehud, the son of Gera, in direct line from Belah, Benjamin's first-born,[4] would lead the delegation responsible for carrying out so delicate a mission.

On the morrow, according to his briefing, he would leave with a party of carriers and make the environs of Jericho, shortly after noon. The day had bristled with activity but now, at last, the official preparations were complete and Ehud slipped back home to handle his personal affairs. There was, he knew, an element of risk. Would he return? He did not know, yet in his heart, a greater hope was burning, than any of the men who sent him knew.

From the start, the tribal elders had insisted that he be obsequious. How he despised the thought. The acceptance of the gift, they said, was wholly paramount to the people's life. The tyrant's favour was imperative. The barest aggravation of the current tribute, could well nigh decimate the tribe.[5] Protocol, they told him, must therefore, be meticulously observed and his feelings of revulsion in the royal presence, held in rein. He must, throughout the period of his audience, whatever his distaste, exhibit all the fawning courtesies expected from the envoy of a vassal state. Ehud had listened with concealed contempt. He heard their words. He knew his duty. It was his honour to fulfil Jehovah's errands. He said no more. With this, the elders seemed content. So darkness fell. The shouting in the courtyard ceased. The carriers agreed their loads. Tomorrow's dawn would see their caravan upon its way . . .

The midnight hour had passed, ere Ehud finally laid down his weapon. He had made it in secret, and he stood with growing pride, surveying his handiwork. Each blade was as sharp as the other and its point like a needle. He turned to his acacia chest and taking out his finest clothing, donned the robes he would wear in the morning. With his usual effort, he tightened the girdle and then with grim intent, fastened his dagger to his right thigh beneath the voluminous folds of his gown. He looked uneasily towards the door and saw that it was bolted. He checked the shutters on the window. They rattled at his touch. He felt resentful of the noise. In deathly silence, the dress rehearsal of his deed began. Hate and fury filled his eyes. His

knuckles whitened with the tension. The blade was out. With
frightening abandon, it cleft the air. How it enraged him! For
almost two decades, the gateway to his tribal hills had been
barred up by Moab's troops at Jericho! Why had the elders
chosen him? He paused a moment. Was it an honour, or must he
view it as his shame? His ancestry was noble, yet he, himself, a
man disabled. His right arm hung mishapen at his side. He felt
it keenly, although his fingers had mobility.[6] He stood there in
the flickering light, the shadows menacing. The wick burned
low. The oil was all but gone. He was a symbol of his nation,
maimed and blighted in a twilight hour. Their right hand, once
so strong, was now as impotent for war as his. Where was The
Captain of Jehovah's hosts? Where The Victor over Jericho?
Why not another triumph there? If God's right hand would
hold his left, then this small dagger would become God's
sword! A carnal frenzy and a living faith joined combat in his
soul. The protocol? He would perform it. The elders' briefing?
He would own it, to the last cool mockery of feigned obeisance.
The niceties achieved, his secret errand would go forward. 'A
message from my God, O king!' So he would word it; and
Eglon, gross in his conceit, was sure to listen, flattered that the
Hebrews' deity should pander to his majesty. Thence to the
sequel. With dagger-quill and tyrant's blood, this page of
history would be written, yes, even though he smudge it with
his own. An ugly relish clouded Ehud's face. Tirelessly, he
thrust and stabbed, as with a ghoulish mien, he danced with
death . . .

Then suddenly the movement ceased. All venom left him.
Limply he knelt to pray. His features calmed. Not by ferocity
but by faith, the alien armies would be vanquished. The
vicious concept of vendetta had always failed to set men free. He
must deliver, but by His Lord's right hand alone. In this
conviction, he retired to rest. The lamp-light spluttered to
extinction. Would all these daring dreams succeed and Israel
hear his trumpet blow?

NOTES

1. Josephus describes Ehud by the Greek word 'neanias', meaning a youth. Chronologically, however, the alternative Jewish tradition is followed in the reconstructive passages of this book. (See the Midrash)
2. Joshua 6 : 26
3. See Judges 1 : 16
4. Cf. Gen. 46 : 21 and Judges 3 : 15
5. The reference to Phinehas, who was a grandson of Aaron and a contemporary of Moses, in Judges 20 : 28, sets the events of Judges, chapters 19 to 21, relating to the massacre of the Benjamites, very early in the chronology of that book. It means that even after approximately one century, the Benjamites of Ehud's day were still not really numerous enough to survive a protracted and rigorous oppression by an alien power. The situation must have been genuinely critical for them and an answer had to be found.
6. The expression, left-handed, applied to Ehud in Judges 3 : 15, is literally, 'shut of his right hand', which seems to imply that he still possessed his right hand but was deprived of the use of it. The fact that he made the dagger, indicates that he could still use his fingers. Many people, however, were left-handed or ambidextrous in Benjamin, as Judges 20 : 16 and I Chronicles 12 : 2 show. Other interesting details of the Ehud story are also found in Judges 3.

Three

Dreams of a Girl

> 'Doth not wisdom cry? and understanding put forth her
> voice?
> 'She standeth in the top of high places ... She crieth
> at the gates, at the entry of the city ... Unto you,
> O men, I call ...
>
> Proverbs 8: 1–4

THE heat was stifling in the royal apartments. How could she
sleep? For hours it seemed, she tossed and turned, listening to
the slightest sound. Now she could hear her father. He was
snoring heavily. Sadly she loathed him; and with each sonorous
tone resounding through the rubble wall, her youthful irrita-
tion grew. No wonder, he and Mother slept apart. 'How fat he
is!' she murmured. Then felt rebuked by her repugnance. He
was, for all his greed, her father.

But Jericho was wretched too! It haunted her, this mausoleum
of splintered rock, that hid the bones of thousands, killed that
day the walls fell flat. She rose, and moved peremptorily,
towards the arch of stone. She trod the sombre portico, illumined
by a single flare and reached the parapet, where guards with
spears strode to and fro. To her this makeshift fortress, built by
her father, whenever Jericho was seized, had always been a
fearful place.[1] Its rooms were grottoes ripe for torture! Assas-
sins lurked in every corner! She viewed her chamber in the keep,
as her retreat from murderous fiends. The balcony on which
she stood, was her escape. Out there the stars looked down. Her
heart flowed out in reverie to meet the distant night. The open
air gave sweet relief. Her slender form relaxed. Her silken
clothes, ungirt, hung loosely from her shoulders to the floor.
About her dusky cheeks, her long black locks lay curling. She
felt alive once more. Fresh sounds came stealing on her ears.

She heard a sharp metallic cry, a night bird calling. The insects chirruped. The tethered beasts below kept stirring. The watch was changed. Each moment breathed its healing quiet. How strong and cool the silence was! She stood alone, one tiny fragment of humanity; a child, whose mother was her only friend in all that world of war. High in the west, the hills of Benjamin and Judah rose steeply in the dark, each naked crag, aglow with starshine. 'Why must they fight?' she wondered, 'Our gods in the valley with their god in the hills.' The glittering deep with sheen of sand gave answer. The Lord of heaven and earth was near.

'But we are Semites too,' she pondered. 'If Israel is of Abraham's seed, we also are of Lot's descendants and therefore of a common stock. What if their herdsmen quarrelled, need such a feud divide us now?' She felt so out of sympathy with everything her father did.[2] If only they could go back east, out of this. sweltering pit of tension: but no, her father would not have it. Regardless of their feelings, she and her mother must be there, these tedious summer weeks in Jericho. To see, she cynically surmised, his great achievements west of Jordan! The whole proud venture was his brain-child. The 'Eglon concept' was to claim the valley, then thrusting always deeper into Israel's heart, make Moabite supremacy secure. 'It is our right!' he liked to bluster, his flabby cheeks in oscillation. 'Lot chose the plain of Jordan! We must possess it! To fail to do so, must betray his name!' Ruth never shared in this conviction, for Israel's God, the God of Abraham, was He who rescued Lot from Sodom. Without that God who answered prayer, there had been no Moab. Yet even so, when Israel came to conquer Canaan, Moab denied their armies food and what is more, their own king Barak chartered Balaam to curse them to a man. Moab had killed them if they could; and now, in spite of all the years, her father still would bleed them dry. The curse was cancelled. Israel was blessed; but could the curse recoil on Moab? Although so young, she had her personal forebodings.

Tired of long standing, the girl leaned quietly forward. Her youthful bosom brushed the stone. Her forearms rested on the wall. Her eyes grew wistful. She was a child, but somehow such a woman now. What did her father know? A guard strode by.

She sensed his presence and his piercing glance. He did not speak. He knew his duty. She was the princess of the realm.[3] She turned her head. Her eyes took in the passing form. She pondered him, so young and resolute; a man. She wished that she had seen his face. At just fifteen, she chose to linger. The guard, no doubt, would pass again. One day, she thought, her father's call would come. Then she would choose; or would she? A sudden dread shot through her frame. What if he forced her? Whom would she marry then? The thing was painfully abhorrent. Her mother filled her aching mind. She could have wept. It hurt to hate, when all her being yearned to love . . .

Now once again her eyes ranged upward to the hills. Out there the dawn was breaking. Her misty fears dissolved. The silvery night broke up before the shining gold of day. How could she know her destiny was in those mountains, forged by the God of heaven, whose heritage her father so bitterly opposed?

NOTES

1. In *The Story of Jericho* by John Garstang M.A., D.Sc., F.S.A. and J. R. E. Garstang M.A. there are to be found these striking observations: 'When was the Fourth City destroyed? (i.e. the Jericho of Joshua's day)' 'It might be thought', they answer, 'that a tell-tale deposit of this graphic character would itself yield up evidence as to the date of this catastrophe. Doubtless much that might have contributed to the solution perished in the fire.' (See Joshua 6 : 24) . . . 'While the Palace itself, being the highest point, was relatively clear, this building was found completely denuded down to its foundations, but in its "layer of destruction" . . . we found a smaller and different structure . . . this house comprised a courtyard and five rooms two of which were much larger than the others . . . It is now clear that the pottery of this "Middle Building" belongs to the second phase of the Late Bronze Age, and the fact that none of it appears in the tombs of the Fourth City, shows that the Middle Building was a later intrusion on the Palace area and shared not at all in the life of the Fourth City. It may indeed have been the residence of Eglon, the Moabite . . .'

   In addition to this information, John Garstang also made further comment in his 'Note on the Revised Date of the Middle Building' in *The American Journal of Semitic Languages and Literature* vol. LVIII no. 4 (October 1941) 'Looking at the plan of this structure, i.e. the Middle Building, we find certain curious features. Though clearly a residence, for it had both hearth and oven, one longroom in the main block was like a stable; and it was provided with its own stout enclosing wall which was laid out noticeably askew from the old lines of the city. What can this strange intrusion signify? To what alien occupier can it be attributed, who secured for his dwelling, the most favoured position on the site, but who apparently made no use of the tombs? The Bible itself provides the answer. In Judges 3 : 12–14 we read: "The Lord strengthened Eglon, the king of

Moab against Israel ... And he gathered unto him the children of Ammon and of Amalek, and went and smote Israel and they possessed The City of Palm Trees, so the children of Israel served Eglon, the King of Moab eighteen years." '

2. The words in Judges 3:12, 'the Lord strengthened Eglon, King of Moab against Israel' do not, of course, express divine sympathy for the Moabite cause. Rather was it the formation of a scourge to discipline His people. As the Lord says later, of Assyria, '. . . the staff in *their* hand is *mine* indignation. I will send him against an hypocritical nation . . .'

3. Amongst Jewish historians there are two distinct traditions regarding the chronology of events recorded in the Book of Ruth. The opening words of the narrative tell us quite plainly it is set in the days of the Judges, but whether at the beginning or the end of that period is very largely a question of conjecture. Josephus, for reasons not disclosed, in his *Antiquities*, Book v, 9.1, maintains that Ruth lived in the days of Eli. This, however, becomes untenable in the light of the inspired comment of Matthew 1:5, where the mother of Boaz is declared to be none other than Rahab. This sets The Book of Ruth, earlier, rather than later in the Judges' period. With this the other Jewish tradition agrees, suggesting quite boldly, that Ruth was actually the daughter of Moabite Eglon. (See the Midrash).

The conclusions of the Garstangs was that the oppression of Israel by Eglon occurred in the reign of Seti I, king of Egypt (1314–1292 B.C.), a period of ineffectual Egyptian control over the Canaanite and trans-Jordan tribal communities. They set the date for the building of Eglon's fortress, 'The Middle Building', round about 1300 B.C. Ruth's appearance at Bethlehem, in this case, would therefore be some thirty years later. Obed was born probably a year afterwards and became, as the Biblical genealogies indicate, the grandfather of David, who was born according to Young soon after 1100 B.C. If we take into account that David was the eighth son of Jesse, and also, that some of the more minor Judges were likely to be contemporary with some of the more prominent Judges of the period, the difficulties of the earlier dating for Ruth, are greatly reduced.

TEN YEARS IN THE FAR COUNTRY

THE FIELDS OF FAMINE

THE TYRANT'S BLOOD

MOVEMENT AND MEN

THE TIME OF THEIR GOING

EBB-TIDE TURNING

THE GREAT DIVIDE

THE PLACE OF MANY WATERS

Now it came to pass in the days when the judges ruled, that there was a famine in the land. And a certain man of Bethlehem-judah went to sojourn in the country of Moab, he, and his wife, and his two sons.

And the name of the man was Elimelech, and the name of his wife Naomi, and the name of his two sons Mahlon and Chilion, Ephrathites of Bethlehem-judah. And they came into the country of Moab, and continued there.

And Elimelech Naomi's husband died; and she was left, and her two sons.

And they took them wives of the women of Moab; the name of the one was Orpah, and the name of the other Ruth: and they dwelled there about ten years.

And Mahlon and Chilion died also both of them; and the woman was left of her two sons and her husband.

Then she arose with her daughters in law, that she might return from the country of Moab: for she had heard in the country of Moab how that the Lord had visited his people in giving them bread.

Wherefore she went forth out of the place where she was, and her two daughters in law with her; and they went on the way to return unto the land of Judah.

And Naomi said unto her two daughters in law, Go, return each to her mother's house: the Lord deal kindly with you, as ye have dealt with the dead, and with me.

The Lord grant you that ye may find rest, each of you in the house of her husband. Then she kissed them; and they lifted up their voice, and wept.

And they said unto her, Surely we will return with thee unto thy people.

And Naomi said, Turn again, my daughters: why will ye go with me? are there yet any more sons in my womb, that they may be your husbands?

Turn again, my daughters, go your way; for I am too old to have an husband. If I should say, I have hope, if I should have a husband also to night, and should also bear sons;

Would ye tarry for them till they were grown? would ye stay for them from having husbands? nay, my daughters; for it grieveth me much for your sakes that the hand of the Lord is gone out against me.

And they lifted up their voice, and wept again: and Orpah kissed her mother in law; but Ruth clave unto her.

And she said, Behold, thy sister in law is gone back unto her people, and unto her gods: return thou after thy sister in law.

And Ruth said, Intreat me not to leave thee, or to return from following after thee: for whither thou goest, I will go; and where thou lodgest, I will lodge: thy people shall be my people, and thy God my God:

Where thou diest, will I die, and there will I be buried: the Lord do so to me, and more also, if ought but death part thee and me.

When she saw that she was stedfastly minded to go with her, then she left speaking unto her.

Four

The Fields of Famine

> '*Is not this the fast that I have chosen? to loose the
> bands of wickedness, . . . then . . . the Lord shall guide
> thee continually, and satisfy thy soul in drought, and
> make fat thy bones . . .*'
>
> Isaiah 58: 6–11
>
> '*Trust in the Lord, and do good; so shalt thou dwell in
> the land, and verily thou shalt be fed.*'
>
> Psalm 37: 3

THE sun that rose that morning to flood all Judah's hills with
light, brought little comfort to Elimelech. His barn like many
another, would soon be empty. The autumn and the winter lay
before him. His future filled with blank despair. He and Naomi
were always struggling. Things might come easily to others
but not to them. Their whole married life had been shadowed
by want, if not of necessities, then of the luxuries they so
passionately craved. Compared with former days, they lived in
much reduced circumstances. This was far from their liking,
yet in spite of their murmurings, they were nowhere near
penniless. They still had their land and certain equipment, but
the crops had been poor and the times were stringent. It was
their memories that goaded them. The peace and plenty of their
youth were hard to forget, for they were born, it would seem,
in the days of Othniel, the first of the Judges. At that time there
was still a measure of order, and people talked of Moses and
Joshua, the glories of the Exodus and the campaigns of conquest. They believed for the most part that Jehovah reigned and
over-ruled in the affairs of the nation. Elimelech's name reflected
that outlook. His father, no doubt, had chosen it specially,
meaning as it does, that 'God is King'. But now after eighteen
long years of Moab's blockade, Elimelech, somehow, found it

hard to believe. He did not deny that their past was authentic
but conditions had changed. The people in Bethlehem were not
like the patriarchs. It was futile to think so. He met them in
business and sat in the gate. With Eglon astride the valleys, it
was not faith, but sheer hard work that had brought them
through. He prided himself that the years of crisis had made him
a realist. The old idea that Canaan flowed with milk and honey
was a myth, as far as he was concerned. It had been a fight all
through, yes, even for their barley and their carob beans.[1]

It was all very well for his relatives to talk, of course; people
like Salmon, Rahab or even their son Boaz. Rahab, as a survivor
from Jericho, was, after all, a bit of a celebrity. She would
hardly be allowed to starve, whatever happened. And as for
Salmon, he was a nephew by marriage, through his Aunt
Elisheba, to Aaron, the original high priest.[2] Such connections
counted, whatever people said. It gave them standing in the
tribe. Then their acreage was large. They could stay solvent in
the direst crisis. It was folk like Naomi and himself that
suffered, left as they were, to their own devices. It was stagger-
ing, mind you, that Salmon ever married Rahab and made the
go of it he did. For one, she was a Gentile; but more than that,
the woman was a harlot before she showed her scarlet thread.
Still, that was Salmon's business. Men make their choices.
Young Boaz, after all, had turned out well. At thirty there was
none to match him. He had a dignity and grace, although
Elimelech disdained his piety. He talked too glibly of his trust
in God. It kind of angered him. Boaz, socially, was upper class,
and for that matter single too. So easy for a man like that to
speak. What cares had he? Peculiar how he had not married. He
was so eligible. Perhaps it was his mother's background.

Elimelech was failing now. His thoughts were forming,
independently of God. The Lord looks on the heart. No doubt
the faith of Rahab, exceeding that of many an Israelite, had
influenced her son profoundly, but few perhaps would think of
that. He turned and looked at Naomi.[3] She never left him un-
affected. Pleasant as her name implied, she moved his heart. Her
age, of late, was more apparent. Faint lines were deepening in
her face and silver strands stole through her jet black hair. It
hurt him when her words were barbed. That never used to be.

Yet how he loved her. She had that charm that only years can bring. Now she concerned him. He could not blame her. Sometimes, he caught her staring sadly at the boys. They were so thin, though both of them were in their teens. Through countless nights, her care had nursed them. Their weakness grieved her and he knew it. A sense of heartbreak filled her eyes. He took her hands, so like his own, dry, cracked and worn through years of labour. He longed to feel their erstwhile softness. But that was gone. Perhaps, far more. Could he be losing her? he wondered. It was a man's reaction. For Naomi, their real relationship was sure. It was the family's need that riled her. Must she be always making do? She felt exhausted with anxiety; too tired to love; too tired to think. Her fears grew stronger. Should she become too tired to care, what then?

The sound of footsteps turned their gaze towards the yard. In through the gate mooched Mahlon and his brother Chilion. Aimlessly, they moped about. They played no games. They did no work. There shone no sparkle in their eyes. They did not laugh. They did not cry. Their listless faces told their story.

'They have no future,' said Elimelech.

'And no incentives!' snapped their mother.

The children's names were witness to their parents' mood. Born in the days when Eglon's grip first brought its blight, their naming spoke of future gloom. Now like the land, both wasted and consumed, they symbolised the current dearth.[4]

'You must do something!' Naomi cried. Without a word, her husband slunk away, wincing within, to seek some unthought plan to break their crisis.

But day by day their cruel dilemma mounted. The famine was their one concern, a topic haunting every meal, each one more meagre than the last. Survival was the endless theme. The heavens were brass, the fields a dustbowl. Prayer lost its meaning. Prices spiralled. His wife and boys must have an answer. The man was frantic. Though near to sacrilege, one day he spoke it.

'Now is the time', he said with fear, 'to sell a section of our field.' A sense of shame at once devoured him. Mar the inheritance? How could he do it?[5] No they must work! Work longer, later; work as they had never done, from sunrise till the stars appeared. That was their only hope; to go on ploughing; to go on sowing. Then, if the furrows proved their grave, at least they'd die in land possessed! It sounded brave, a little like he used to be, before his faith had been eroded.

But Naomi had had enough. She could not traffic in delusion. No load of work could solve their problem. They had to act.

'Why stop at that?' she dared to ask him. 'I'd sell the lot, then emigrate!' Her depression was critical and distorted her judgment. Her exasperation was out of character and Elimelech felt more alarmed. To sell and stay was hard enough; but to sell and go was something he had never mooted. He felt stunned at the prospect.

'But this is our inheritance,' he protested, 'and Bethlehem-judah is our home. All our relatives are here. Wherever would we go?

'I haven't the slightest notion,' replied Naomi. 'All I know is, we can't stay here, that's all!'

At first the idea seemed preposterous but as the sense of shock receded, it gained some credence in his mind. Try to escape? He had not thought of that! True, they had fought it long enough. The thing, initially impossible, might yet prove feasible; but they would need some opening to the south or east . . .

The will to fight soon dies, when once the wish to flee is born. How far from God they were, they did not know. The distance would be measured soon by wayward feet. Decisions are not babes in arms but ageing children come to wedlock. Peace lies, not in our strategems, but in the Strategist on high. Man puts such score on changed environment. It is redemption that he needs. We make our problems, God His plans. A wavering faith flirts first with folly then finally makes fate its mate.

Who now could stop them in their course? The road to ruin had begun.

NOTES

1. Barley and carob beans were the staple food of the poor.
2. See Exodus 6: 23 with Ruth 4: 20–21. This connection tends to confirm the early dating of The Book of Ruth in the Judges period.

3. Naomi means 'pleasant', 'lovely' or 'delightful'.
4. Mahlon means 'sick' or 'wasting'. Chilion means 'pining' or 'consumption'. Morris asserts, 'these names were found at Ugarit, so they are . . . old Canaanite names'. It shows, perhaps, pagan influence already at work in their parents.
5. Although this passage is imaginative, yet it depicts the horror of the Israelite disposing of the inheritance of his fathers with no immediate prospect of redeeming it, or of its soon release in the year of Jubilee which only recurred every fifty years. Naboth's view in I Kings 21 : 3 is typical, and is recorded favourably.

Five

The Tyrant's Blood

'Sin shall not have dominion . . .'
Romans 6: 14

'. . . the haft also went in after the blade.'
Judges 3: 22

IN the grey hours of that selfsame dawn, Ehud's column of men
and beasts picked their way, down through the defiles, from
Mount Ephraim to The City of Palm Trees. The sun rose from
a purple bed of crumpled hills, which stretched like a quilt of
ebony and flame, all the way to the horizons of Moab. Radiant
peaks, bright with the day, crowned savage faults still harbour-
ing shadows of the night; whilst far below, a writhing swathe of
green defined the presence of the Jordan. The mules kicked up
the dust. The drovers scrambled with the loads. The gradient
and the heat increased. The fiery air dried up their sweat. The
caravan strung out. The handling of the beasts was more
desultory. The naked rock glowered cruelly down and thorn-
barbed scrub marked all their way. The hours slipped by and
Ehud made them slacken pace. The forward sentinels could
halt them soon. The challenge came. They proffered the agreed
credentials. All proved in order. Prior notice had averted
skirmish. They crossed the Moab lines unharmed.

Under surveillance, the descent continued. The men fell
silent. Ehud rode on, his eyes alert. They swept the landscape,
noting every nook for cover. Not since his boyhood had he seen
this country. The whole terrain bespoke an anguish. Contorted
rock and twisted stone wept, in some places, with a sickly slime,
and here and there, the sunbleached salt gave ghostliness to
cliff and stack. Lizards, their throats a-pulse, soaked up the sun,
then scattered at the sound of feet. The zigzags straightened.

The long decline splayed out in screes, as if to grasp the valley floor. Not much had changed, though fort-like dwellings lined approaches and crude defences scarred the hills. They rounded one more bluff of rock and there King Eglon's fortress stood. It rose in rough-hewn stone upon the knoll that once was Jericho. It looked, to Ehud's eyes, as ugly as its infamy implied, yet set amidst a splash of green, found borrowed splendour. Neat watered fields lay fringed with palms to give a sense of rich oasis. Black goats cropped keenly at the coarse-leafed grasses. The beasts of burden paused to drink. So did the men. The air was tropical. All was oppressive. The porters found it hard to breathe. It felt like noon.[1]

Then came the palace escort, with steeds that bore the royal insignia. Five furlongs from the fort, Ehud was motioned to dismount. As envoy of a vassal state, he must not ride, but walk becomingly to meet the king. Slowly, and with measured tread, he marched bare-headed in the scorching sun. The final stretch inclined quite steeply to the gates. He felt so unaccustomed to the heat and perspiration blurred his vision. Within the ramparts, they were halted. The mules, once tethered in the yard, were quickly lightened of their treasure. The household steward fussed and fumed, till all were suitably assembled. Then Ehud at the appointed word, was granted audience. His carriers followed, each with his gift held high, conveyed with servile pomp and draped with gold.

Up on the battlements, the princess Ruth, talked with her mother. Hearing the sound of hooves and voices, she lent across the parapet and peered below.

'A Hebrew embassage,' her mother said. 'See how they dress. I heard they would be down today. They come from Benjamin. Wanting something, I expect, as usual. I wouldn't trust them for a moment!' She paused then added with some bitterness, 'Your father loves that kind of thing! I don't!'

As always in the heat of summer, King Eglon held his court inside the screened north portico.[2] It was the coolest corner of the building and he preferred it there. In fact he had designed the area with this end in view. He found his obesity intolerable in the high humidity, but in the portico, was able both to rest and work. Ruth watched the puny leader enter. To her he looked a bit deformed. She watched the porters as they followed. How curious she was to see those gifts. 'They will be beautiful,' she mused. 'Their craftsmanship is so exquisite. Could not her father think of her? Perhaps, this once? A little jewelry for a wasted summer was surely not too much to ask?' A few short minutes and out the party trooped again. She saw them hustled to the kitchens, where after some brief meal, they would, no doubt, be packed off promptly to the mountains.

Suddenly the gong was sounding. 'I better take something,' she said, indifferently. 'Then I must rest.' She had been longing for a siesta all the morning, after that broken night . . .

How long she slept she did not know but when she awoke, she saw a guard, fully armed, standing at her bedside. She looked at his face and somehow did not question his intrusion. His eyes were anxious. He seemed familiar. The western sun streamed strongly through the narrow windows. Her heart beat faster. 'What do you want?' she said with growing apprehension. Their eyes met searchingly. The youth stood hesitant. His lip was quivering. 'Your Highness,' he said, 'It is my duty to inform you that the Glory of Moab is laid low.' He waited and the silence lengthened, as if his words had failed to register.

'You don't mean my father . . .?' began Ruth.

'Yes,' he said softly, 'it was the envoy from Benjamin.'

'Not that little man,' she gasped, 'I saw him go.' Then she burst into tears. The young guard reached forward to comfort her and would have kissed her, but he restrained himself.

'You must flee now,' he said urgently. 'Dress quickly, and warmly too! You could be up all night. Your mother's waiting in the hall below. You need to reach the Jordan in the next half hour. The revolt is on. They are coming like jackals down the mountains!'

The guard withdrew. She watched his figure pass beyond the arch, as one half mesmerised. 'Be quick!' he shouted, glancing back. 'The time is short!'

Dazed and confused, she jumped from her couch, tightened her girdle and slipped her necklace and her bangles on. Awake at last, and alive to the danger, she sped down the stairway, a whirl of youthful agility and girlish alarm straight into the arms of her mother. She was trembling with shock as her daughter clasped her. Beyond her heaving shoulder, Ruth glimpsed the horses in the courtyard. The shadows of their legs looked long, she thought, the dogs uneasy. Then all at once she saw the saddles. She knew the bodyguard were waiting. They crossed the yard, like soldiers wounded in the battle. She saw the guard once more and he saluted.

'Can you not come?' Ruth whispered, as they passed.

'I must act on my orders,' he answered.

The party cantered eastward to the river. He watched them dwindle, till all were lost amidst the sand-scoured hills. He would remember her, not in her fears, but standing nobly in the strrlight. A harsh command stabbed through his thinking. He turned abruptly and obeyed. The bliss and sorrow blurred together. The bloodshed followed. There was no meeting over Jordan.

Late in the afternoon, the royal mourners reached the crossing. Being summertime, the waters were clear and the drooping willows, and the tamarisks, gave to the fording-place a haunting loveliness. The water level was tolerably low, so dispensing with the military raft, they passed over on horseback without difficulty. They felt they dare not rest, so pressed on farther, making for Ruth's favourite valley, where in season, the brambles mingle with the oleanders, and the red brown foliage of the pomegranate lends beauty to the fig trees fresh and green. Slowly they climbed, their silence stonier than the rocks beneath them. The vegetation thinned, then petered out and once again they came to sand. They reached the heights and turned, instinctively, to look in dread, towards the crossing. Only an hour had passed but what a carnage! Like angered hornets, the Hebrew tribesmen fanned out along Jordan. Thousands upon thousands there were, all armed to the teeth, with scythes and axes, spears and cudgels. The valleys were alive with men. In frenzied mobs they slaughtered Eglon's forces dispersing to the river. Not one escaped. Relentlessly they slashed and bludgeoned, tossing the senseless bodies, dead or dying, down into the flowing waters. The quiet meandering Jordan blushed deep crimson in the sunset, a blood-stained epitaph to dreams turned nightmare. The pent up outrage of the long, hard years erupted in unbridled violence. 'The haft,' as

with Ehud, 'went in after the blade.' The sight was withering.
They could not really bear to look, yet went on looking. As in a
trance, Ruth stood impassive unable to indulge the right emotion. Her mother fell again to sobbing, her face distorted as she
fought her feelings.

'It happened in the portico,' she muttered, gulping her tears.
Ruth did not speak, but listened stone-like to the garbled words.
'No one', she said, 'seemed to know how he did it. O that ugly
little wretch from Benjamin. If only I could lay hands on him!'

'He did come back then?' queried Ruth. But her words seemed
distant; as if another person spoke them. She looked again at the
horses. Their eyes were glassy and their nostrils dilated. Two
of them began to whinny. Fear is infectious. Ruth felt so
baffled by her mother. What was it that she mourned? Her lost
position or her murdered husband? Faint love weeps loudly in
bereavement.

'O yes,' she answered, 'he came back all right! He craved a
second audience of the King. Needless to say, your father gave
it. You know what he was like. Never missed anything if he
could help it! And the man was so "courteous", the officers
told me. And so insignificant! He had a message from God, he
said. Did you ever hear the like of it? Well, your father fell for it
and made the guardsmen withdraw. After that no one could tell
me what happened. The stupidity of men just staggers me! The
blood was dreadful, they said. They'd never seen such blood
but they couldn't find the weapon!' A devilish anger filled her
tear-stained face. 'Those Benjamites were always liars. What
filthy brigands, the whole vile lot of them!' She paused, then
said with bitterness. 'Well, little princess, you and I are future-
less now!' It was just as Ruth thought.

'But maybe he did have a message?' Ruth ventured, hardly
weighing her words.

'What do you mean?' screamed her mother. 'What *do* you
mean?'

'A message from God!' said Ruth. 'He writes in blood,
sometimes. Isn't that what the sages say?' Her mother's hysteri-
cal reaction deeply disturbed her. There followed a desperate
silence. And she felt she could never be forgiven. 'I was thinking
of the curse,' she explained. 'You know the curse,' she said.

'What curse?' asked her mother.

'There is only one curse,' was the answer.[3]

Distraught, the soldiers reined their horses and the two rode on towards oblivion, each with their thoughts and each with their woes.

*   *   *   *   *

It was already dusk when other riders came galloping through the gates of Bethlehem. The sound of their hooves on the cobbles drew startled glances, from the windows. They rapidly dismounted and immediately their news was out. One look at their mounts foaming wildly at the mouth, told its importance. Just minutes later Mahlon and Chilion burst in on Naomi. 'Eglon's dead!' they shouted, 'Eglon's dead! And our men are going down to Jordan! O let us go, Mother; do let us go!' She was quite dumbfounded at their jubilant report.

'But is it true?' she asked, with motherly caution.

'Of course it's true,' replied the youngsters, with that confidence so typical of youth.

'Go and find your father, then,' she told them. and off they scampered, more excited than she had ever seen them.

Needless to say, Mahlon and Chilion did not go to Jordan; at least not then. They were still far from robust and as yet, rather young for the venture; but had they known, the day was not far distant when they would cross its waters.

It was a month or two later when they moved. Once Elimelech and Naomi had finally decided, they foreclosed their limited affairs, and made tracks for Moab. In the changed circumstances, it was to be just a short term project, so they did not sell their land. The plan was to go down into the newly occupied areas and share in the fruits of victory. There would be plenty to eat in Moab. Their granaries would be full, and they as Israelites, amongst the conquerors. Men would be scarce in Moab, too, after the massacre and there would be good openings for the boys. Once the economy of Ephratah and the surrounding district had recovered, they would return to the heights and make a fresh start. Meanwhile, it seemed pointless to face another year or two's hardship in Bethlehem. Better surely, to go to the valley till the tide of plenty and the renewal of crops had returned to Judah. The change would surely do them good.

It was not as if they were really leaving the inheritance. They still retained it!

So like Abraham and Isaac, in their day, who left The Land and courted loss,[4] Elimelech quits Bethlehem, the house of bread, and Judah, the heritage of praise.[5] Behind the narrative of Scripture and the ancient histories, we have the inklings of their story, and a fleeting glimpse of Ruth's romance. The details that we know are sparse. Antiquity shows but few her secrets; yet if the outline here suggested, gives something of a real-life sense, it may still serve to rouse to interest. God's purposes run on through all the ebb and flow of power. The Book of Ruth starts with Elimelech. His name declares that 'God is King'. It closes with another man, who proves to be the king God chose. God's sovereignty and saving acts are not divided. From anarchy, His monarchy comes forth. Mankind may fail but He remains our kinsman still.

NOTES

1. *The Bible as History* by Werner Keller, translated from the German by William Neil, M.A., B.D., Ph.D., gives on pp. 158–159 this informative note on the area above described.

   "The Jordan basin has a tropical climate. The village of Eriha, the modern successor of Jericho, gives the impression of being an oasis on the edge of a barren waste of chalk. Even palms grow here, although they are seldom seen anywhere else in Palestine, except to the south of Gaza. The Bible, too, calls Jericho, 'The City of Palm Trees' (Judges 3 : 13). Golden red clusters of dates shimmer among the green foliage. From ancient times, the spring called Ain es Sultan has produced, as if by magic, this lush patch of vegetation. North of present day Jericho, a mound of ruins is named after it, Tell es-Sultan . . . In this mound under the strata of the Bronze Age, lie traces of the Stone Age . . . In 1953, a British expedition conducted excavations here and the director of the enterprise, Dr. Kathleen M. Kenyon declared, "Jericho can lay claim to being by far the oldest city in the world." "

2. This area is described as a 'summer parlour' in Judges 3 : 20, which means 'a roof-chamber'. It was possibly a verandah room built out over columns supporting the building where the land fell away. It could on the other hand have been on the flat roof itself, but hardly so, if the fortress were any height; for Ehud seems to have slipped away without arousing one suspicion.

3. It is interesting in this connection to read Numbers 21 : 29–30, where it says, 'Woe to thee Moab! Thou art undone, O people of Chemosh!'

4. See Genesis 12 : 10–20; 16 : 3; 25 : 12, regarding Abraham; and Genesis 26 : 1–11 regarding Isaac. Note the specific command of God to Isaac not to go down into Egypt but to dwell in the land. 'Sojourn in the land,' He says, 'and I will bless thee,' and then follows an exhortation and promise

coupled with the re-iteration of the Abrahamic Covenant, regarding the seed and the inheritance.

5. Bethlehem means, 'the place of food'; 'the house of bread'; or even a 'granary'. Judah means 'praise'. The placing of the city and tribal location together distinguished this Bethelehem from the one in Zebulun, mentioned in Joshua 19: 15.

Six

Movement and Men

'When the Lord raised them up judges, then the Lord
was with the judge, and delivered . . . them all the days
of the judge.'
                                                    Judges 2: 18
'He ever liveth to make intercession.'
                                                    Hebrews 7: 25

THE narrative of The Book of Ruth begins with a familiar
formula of words. 'Now it came to pass in the days of the
judges . . .' This is a phrase occurring no less than five times in
Scripture,[1] that is with the exception of the last three words.
Each time it is indicative of a period of impending adversity,
which by reason of divine deliverance, issues in a happier outcome. This mode of introducing the story should therefore
heighten expectation. It should make us look for the works of
God in this era, so painfully fraught with the works of men. Like
the parables that Jesus told, the Old Testament stories are all
narrated from God's standpoint, for the Bible is history, as God
conceives it; the things on earth, as written in the books of
heaven. History is not so much the fortunes of human dynasties
but the realisation of divine destinies. It is not controlled by the
revolution of the underdog but by the intervention of The
Supreme. It is not the outcome of contradictory economic
forces in society, but the operation of the dynamic forces of
Deity. History is The Eternal active in Time.

The days of the Judges were days of stubborn departure
from God, which brought to Israel subjugation from without
and a frightening starvation at home. Her infidelity soon spawned
idolatry, and idolatry, the basest of immorality. It was a course
that could not be followed with impunity. Changing the glory
of the incorruptible God into the image of corruptible man and

creeping things, God gave them up to uncleanness; exchanging the truth of God for a lie, God gave them up to vile affections; and not wishing to retain God in their knowledge, God gave them up to a reprobate mind.[2] Of Egypt's pride, we read, 'the horse and the rider hath He thrown into the sea'. Israel was out of Egypt, but Egypt and its gods, together with the Canaanite abominations, were still in Israel. The twelve tribes were like a team of headstrong horses that would not be turned and were thus plunging headlong down to Egypt's fate. God would ride them to victory but they would not have Him. He was casting, therefore, the reins over their heads. In some degree, Paul's descriptive phrase, 'God gave them up', which occurs three times in Romans one, describes their predicament. In Israel's case, however, this was never a total abandonment. For a while He allowed them their wild career, knowing full well, that the wounds received in their flight from His governance would oblige them to pause and consider. When they were ready to return, the days of desolation became days of salvation. God stepped in and raised up a deliverer. The days of the Judges, consequently, are not simply concerned with the evil of man and the failure of Israel, but the goodness of God that leads to repentance. Without His intervention, Israel would have been extinguished and they would have had no history. So it has been all down the centuries. God stepping in, infuses history with a content. Again and again we see it happen. God broods on the waters, and order springs out of chaos; He saves Noah's household from the flood and preserves our race; He calls out Abram from idolatry, and through his seed, obtains a bridge-head on the earth. God gives His Law and makes His covenants. He establishes ordinances and sends His prophets. He comes in Christ. He is Light shining in the darkness. He is God bringing life out of death. He makes a way where there is no way, and a fountain for cleansing through the blood of His cross. He bestows His Spirit. He fashions His bride. He changes men, and goes on changing them. He plants His churches, He sways the nations, He fulfils His will. He heads up everything. He is the Source and Goal of all phenomena. He works at the beginning. He works to His end. He is the First and the Last, the Great Inaugurator, Prosecutor, and Completer; God, all in all.

The early history of Israel, as Ridout and Darby taught, is
clearly illustrative of the chequered history of the Church.
During the days of Joshua and throughout the lifetime of those
leaders who knew him, Israel to some degree, followed the
Lord, but after their death, a swift decline set in. This tide of
evil was only stemmed by God-sent men like the Judges, who,
clothed with His Spirit, stood rock-like, against the sinister
currents of the times. To such leaders the people rallied; and as
repentance and renewal laid hold on them, the insurgent forces
of evil and pressure of alien cultures were thrown back. This
alternating experience of defeat and victory continued, until at
last, the triumphs of David and the peace of Solomon brought in
God's Kingdom and set His Throne in Zion.

The parallel is evident. All the days that Jesus, the final
Joshua, was on earth, and during the lifetime of His apostles,
the believers were largely loyal to their Master, but once they
were gone, the Church like Israel in her day, succumbed to the
inroads of unbelief, pagan worship and pernicious heresy.
Moral standards quickly declined and soon the distinction
between Christ's Church and the world was utterly blurred.
But once again as in the case of Israel, God raised up Spirit-
filled men, who, in the Church, stood against the flood of
wickedness. Such are the great reformers and emancipators, the
outstanding evangelists and teachers of the Word, who, in their
generation, transformed the scene. As the period covered by the
Books of Joshua, Judges and Ruth issued in the inauguration
of God's Kingdom at the hand of David and his son, so the
vicissitudes of Church history, will be followed by God's
millenial Kingdom, vested in great David's greater Son, that is
in Jesus Christ. This will not be accomplished, however, by the
Church's influence, anymore than Israel was able to produce
God's Kingdom. All they produced in their apostasy, was King
Saul, a 'type' of the Antichrist. The Kingdom in their day was
brought in by one who severed Goliath's head. So in a coming
day, Christ will reign, not by reason of any Church achieve-
ment, but through His own prowess, who, single-handed,
bruised the serpent's head and annulled his works. The ways of
God, therefore, with the Israelites, Elimelech and Naomi; and
with Ruth, the Gentile believer, who was brought into the

inheritance of God through grace, has much to say to us, who
are believers from amongst the Gentiles today.[3] The sovereignty
of God is a bulwark for faith in every age. 'What I do,' said
our Lord to Peter, 'thou knowest not now, but thou shalt know
hereafter.' In the climax of the ages, we too shall say that all that
befell us was of His mercy; and the realised goal, the final
evidence of grace.

Whichever way, then, we look at things, be it personally or
universally, the clue to the meaning of life remains the same.
God stepping into a life; God stepping into a nation; God
stepping into the world is the source of all significance here.
The way a man reacts to God's movements defines his role in
the world arena. He may be for Him; he may be against Him,
but God will sense his least resistance and His first acceptance.
At times, a certain case is written in His Book, The Bible. It
was so with the man, Elimelech. Many were the footsteps on the
road he took, but his were different. He was caught in a movement of events and things that quite transcended his discerning.
God describes him as 'a certain man'. His planned migration is of
consequence, not only to himself and family but to posterity. He
is heedless, but God is measuring all his steps. All that he has
and is, dissolves; yet unity pervades confusion. God's strategy
is running through. As in a tangled ball of wool, there is one
thread we need to find, so God's own Spirit picks it out and
shows it to us in this story. Man's wilfulness may work out to its
last wild bite, but God will still achieve His plans. Elimelech
may choose, but God will not be turned aside. Elimelech
may go to Moab, aspiring to the seeming 'best' and there
expire, but God will bring Ruth out of Moab, and grant her
living seed in Bethlehem. 'God is not mocked.' Satan first
attacked the woman, but in her seed his doom was sealed.
Pharoah drowned the baby boys. He used the river for his
purpose, but one babe from that very river, ravaged all his land
and nation. Haman raised his gallows, to do away with Mor-
decai, but Haman was the man they hanged. The Jews he
hated were preserved. His own large family were wiped out.
Satan, through Herod, killed the innocents. The very Innocent
he missed, prevailed against him at the last. The departures of
men are impotent to foil God's ends. They only serve them. The

way out for Elimelech meant a way in for Ruth. The unbelief
of Israel gives a door of faith to the Gentiles. The cross was
Satan's masterpiece, but by that cross, Christ mastered Satan.
The 'irony of fate' becomes the alchemy of God. From earthen
circumstance, He brings His own eternal gold.

The Book of Ruth then, declares God's purpose and proclaims it immutable. As standing between Israel's rejection of
the theocracy under Moses and Joshua, and the divine insti-
tution of the monarchy under David and Solomon, it traces the
appointed lineage, right through to a 'rod which sprang from the
stem of Jesse'. Not only so; it speaks of precious things preserved, of honour, reverence, faith, and chastity, in times of
breakdown. God's things still flourish where His stream flows
through. They blossom as a fragrant rose in hostile sands. It
tells of sweet submission to God's will and that by humble
womenfolk, when anarchy was all the vogue. God's root is
vibrant here. It forms a green oasis in the waste of years. The
springs of God's salvation break forth gladly. He is at work,
and takes us first to Bethlehem. This is the place He so much
treasures. His visitation there begins. Its much loved well was
ever His. But God's attention portends crisis. In Scripture,
Bethlehem *is* critical. Review the events that cluster round it.
We find it a city of coming and going, of life and death, of
hopes and fears; a place of birth and departure; of anguish and
delirious joy. There Benjamin arrives and Rachel goes. Elimelech vacates, and Ruth moves in. Mahlon and Chilion go
forth and perish. Obed is nursed, and the ageing Naomi lives
again. David's men risk all to serve him; a cup of water in his
name. There Jesus is born. His star is shining; yet countless
little children die. The angels praise, the shepherds worship,
then mother's eyes flow down with tears.

And so we mark the way this 'certain man' is taking. He goes
in silence.[4] God probes him but he gives no answers. To use
the well-worn phrase, 'Elimelech is not available for comment'.
Yet does the runaway escape? We are our own conundrums.
We will not think before we sink but carry all our burdens with
us. The questions in our conscience goad us. Our very constitu-
tion breaks us, once we are outward bound from God. All hope
of happiness is forfeit. It always is, if 'our way' wins. We call it

honey and we count it sweet. But how we sicken, as we eat
without Him. Of Hagar God demands, 'Whence camest thou,
and whither wilt thou go?' And of Elijah on Mount Horeb,
'What doest thou here?' Of Jonah in the tossing boat, 'What
meanest thou?' Of Saul of Tarsus, midst the pricks, 'Why
persecutest thou Me?' Such persons on 'their way' are shattered
by His dread encounter. There is no answer to such basic
questions, save in submission. Elimelech had chosen to abandon Bethlehem, God's house of bread. For him there could be
no solution. He trod the way out and thus the way down. He
went with his Naomi but without his true Lover. This was his
tragedy for none but His God could provide a way through.

NOTES

1. See Ruth 1: 1; Genesis 14: 1; Esther 1: 1; Isaiah 7: 1; Jeremiah 1: 3
2. See Romans 1: 18–32
3. See Romans 9: 12–36
4. In the Book of Ruth there are no words of Elimelech recorded.

Seven

The Time of Their Going

> 'The ox knoweth his owner, and the ass his master's crib: but Israel doth not know, my people doth not consider.'
>
> Isaiah 1 : 3
>
> 'Yea, the stork in the heaven knoweth her appointed times; and the turtle and the crane and the swallow observe the time of their coming; but my people know not the judgment of the Lord.'
>
> Jeremiah 8 : 7
>
> 'A certain man went down ... to Jericho, and fell among thieves ...'
>
> Luke 10 : 30

THERE were two main routes across the hills from Bethlehem to the Jordan valley. One lay due east across the rugged unfrequented country lying between the town of Bethlehem and the Dead Sea. Since Lot separated from Abraham, few if any Hebrew communities had settled in that part of the country, which now pertained to Judah. There is little doubt therefore, when the choice was made, that Elimelech took the more northerly route on his way to Moab. To follow any other road, was to risk his family on rough unguarded trails, across hills, where pockets of alien tribesmen might still be hiding.

Although they left with no small measure of resolution, it was, nevertheless, with mixed feelings that Elimelech and Naomi turned their backs on the family home. Bethlehem-judah still meant a great deal to them. They had their fields there yet. The trouble was, it did not mean enough; and so they went. Mahlon and Chilion on the other hand, never had a second thought. Through lack of proper emphasis at home, they were already conditioned for the Moabite scene. Mere neglect of young hearts gives them up to the world. They viewed the journey as the greatest diversion. In fact, Naomi could not remember her sons so elated. The whole venture had put new zest into them. Early one morning they slipped away. Farewells had all been said. They preferred that none should see them when they finally departed. They felt self-conscious; so no one came to say, 'God-speed'. Before the little town had stirred, the parents and their boys were gone. They needed all the time, they said, to get to Jordan. The course they took was all worked out; the route, the loads and the provisions. They hoped to make Beth Hoglah[1] as the sun went down. They took no risks, except the biggest risk of all. Their 'chance of a life time', must prove but a death-march. Moab grew larger every hour. Israel diminished; till once across the frontier, their only world *was* Moab. And worse than that, Moab, itself, became 'their Israel'. Eglon was dead! They were free to enjoy themselves; or so they thought. As some at Rome once said, 'Let us continue in sin, that grace may abound'.

Beyond the north gate, the road fell quickly away and they turned, almost without thinking, to look once more at their native place. There was Bethlehem, already old, perched on the heights, her sunlit terraces of flat-roofed dwellings clinging tenaciously to the crown of the hill. Here and there tall cypress trees, like tapering fingers, pointed skyward in the morning light. Downward they stumbled, barely conscious of a lone stone pillar marking the spot of a wayside tomb. This was the place where Rachel died. Could there be idols in her heart? 'Call him Benoni!' she cried in anguish, 'Son of my sorrow!' 'No! Call him Benjamin,' cried Jacob, 'Son of my right hand!' They pressed on regardless; nor did they recall that Ehud, left-handed and a Benjamite, had been God's right hand man at Jericho. The little caravan moved on, until they reached the Hebron junction. They took, as previously agreed, the northward arm to Jerusalem, the ancient stronghold of the Jebusites. Although in Joshua's day reduced by sword and fire, some lived there still, mingling illicitly with Benjamin's seed.[2] Once past the parting of the ways, they took the trail along the lofty ridge that looks out westward on the Vale of Rephaim. The ancient city rose before them. They did not enter, but skirting by the Valley of Hinnom, they turned off eastward across the sun-kissed flanks of Olivet. This brought them out at Enshe-mesh, from whence the waters pour down to Enrogel. From there they crossed just one more ridge to Adummim, which lies above the road over against Geliloth. Then descending rapidly, they passed on by the Stone of Bohan,³ until they came down into the Valley of Jordan. They could see the river before them now, and away to the north, through the fields, the tyrant Eglon's derelict fortress. Its tumbled stone, in the setting sun, was alive with mystery. Young Mahlon and Chilion thrilled with adventure. It had been a great day, coming through the mountains, and now the tropical scenes of the Jordan ravine filled them with wonder. Like youngsters in any generation, the immediate consumed them. Death seemed so distant, when life was calling.

The following morning they forded the river, which only eight weeks earlier ran with blood. On reaching the eastern bank, they contacted officers of the occupying Israelite forces, with a view to obtaining a holding in the country. Many of the farms lay vacant, with fruit unpicked in the orchards, and live-stock grazing unattended. The massacre had left the male population of Moab much depleted, especially near the river and many of the women and children had fled to the wadis. In a secluded and prosperous valley, well back from the Jordan, they were finally allocated an excellent property. There was no one about and they simply moved in. It was like the halcyon days of the first occupation of Canaan, when God gave them 'great and goodly cities they did not build and houses full of all good things which they did not fill, and wells which they did not dig and vineyards and olive trees they did not plant'. Had they thought of those words which Moses wrote,⁴ they might have remem-bered the warning that went with them, for he continues, 'Beware lest thou forget the Lord which brought thee forth . . . from the house of bondage. Thou shalt fear the Lord thy God, and serve Him. Ye shall not go after the gods of the people which are round about you . . . lest the anger of the Lord thy God be kindled against thee, and destroy thee from off the face of the earth.'

The occupation forces were glad of any civilian backing they could get from their own people. It made their position more secure. Thus Elimelech and Naomi received all the encouragement they needed to make a success of their new venture. It made them feel they were doing the right thing, but sad to say, it was all undertaken with the wrong motives. It is one thing to be in Moab as a soldier claiming the promises[5] but quite another as a self-seeker, with one's own devices. The biggest bugbear now, was the heat, though in one sense, it was a welcome change from the bleakness of the hills, where sleet, and even snow, could fall in winter.

Mahlon and Chilion grew to manhood. The local folk slowly regained their confidence and drifted back to the countryside. The animosities of earlier days receded and many of the widowed women proved only too ready to work in the fields and thus procure a livelihood for their orphaned children. Ruth, and her mother who, it would seem, eventually remarried,[6] mingled with the district peasantry, and Ruth first learned of harvest there. If the old tradition of Ruth's parentage be true, the Scripture maintains silence on her links with Eglon. But this is understandable. Her past association with the crushed regime would hardly come to light at such a time as this, for fear of what might happen, if the truth were known. Whatever may have been the case, somewhere in Moab's fields, Mahlon came in touch with Ruth. From the early awakenings of her womanhood and the desolation of her entire background, Ruth had known the terror of loneliness. After the bloodbath she had witnessed from the hill, her land seemed only to contain old men, young children and heartbroken women. Where could she go? What could she do? It is hardly surprising, that when Mahlon and his parents showed an interest in her, that she responded, Hebrew 'conquerors' though they were. No doubt she longed for real security. Perhaps she longed for something more. Maybe a link with the seed of Abraham, and the living God, to her, as yet, so dimly known.

Before the day of the wedding, the first of a whole series of crippling tragedies struck at Naomi. She had never thought it could happen to her. All was going so well. They were nicely settled now in Moab. The privations of the famine in Bethlehem were well behind them and for the first time in their married life, they were beginning to feel prosperous. No one ever suggested returning. The tiny piece of land up there on the mountains was all but forgotten and its spiritual significance discounted. Their earlier misgivings had tended to disperse and their erstwhile sojourn had lengthened to a permanent stay. The Scripture tells us of this development and gives an inference of their changed psychology. What, in the first place, we do with grave concern, is later done with verve and nonchalance; until at last the means we used, are 'justified' by ends attained. When first they went, it was 'to sojourn' and that infers 'to be a stranger'. But then we read how they 'came there' and 'continued there'. Till finally we are told 'they dwelt there'. This last phrase means 'to sit down'. They were taking root in foreign soil. But how could it nourish them? Then suddenly Elimelech died. The ground on which he chose to live, opened now to receive his remains. O bitter death in that far-off country! Having failed to trust in his father's God, his bones are not gathered to his father's tomb. His epitaph would be his name. Yes, God was King. In life he denied it, but his grave declared it.[7] God is not mocked. We can only exclaim at the tomb of Elimelech, 'It is of the Lord's mercies, we are not consumed.'

When Elimelech died, something shrivelled inside Naomi. Cut off from her relatives in Israel, an alien in Moab and her sons espoused to local girls, she felt a woman apart, sadly forsaken and very old, though barely fifty yet. With her husband gone, the burden of the farm fell on the boys. Mahlon and Ruth soon married and so did Chilion and Orpah. The girls were willing workers but it was not long, before they realised just how much Elimelech had done. Naomi, as the months passed by, tried to regain her cheerfulness but without success. She was not really averse to Ruth and Orpah. They were very kind to her and even loved her. She sensed that, in a host of ways. Of the two, Ruth was not so much attached to the local deities as Orpah, so gave her little concern, but Chilion's wife caused her great anxiety. Gradually her little images were installed in the courtyard. Then one by one, they began to find their way into the house, until they sat there on the shelf for all to see. Mahlon and Chilion were what they called, 'open-minded'. They did not see that it mattered, having no faith of their own. If Orpah wanted it that way and derived some comfort from her gods, they were not going to interfere. Naomi had tried to say something when it all started but had felt so silenced. What could she say? She had been out of touch with God's people for years. She was far from Jehovah and now utterly compromised. Through her estrangement from the Lord, her boys had never learned to love Him. She dimly remembered that the Books of Moses frowned on such marriages as theirs, yet she had connived at their union with these unbelievers. Had she forgotten the affair of Baal-peor?[8] Why, Moabite offspring were debarred from the congregation, till the tenth generation![9] She had no copy of the Law to which she might refer. There was no priest of Aaron's sons with whom to take counsel; and no place of sacrifice for sins. The fault was all with her. How could she blame her sons, much less their wives?

Gradually, the demands of married life, the daily pressure of work and the constant managing of the farm in the hot, humid climate, began to tell on Mahlon and Chilion. They had never been strong; and unused to responsibility as they were, the handling of the livestock and the crops became increasingly onerous. Ruth and Orpah, being natives of those parts, kept going with their usual vigour. Their husbands, with their waning strength could only feel the more embarrassed. They drove themselves beyond their measure. Inherent weakness brought them low. The slightest illness gave alarm. First one and then the other took to bed. Each in their turn just slipped away. The farm came quickly to a standstill. Disconsolately, their graves were dug beside their father's sepulchre. The braying donkeys and the bleeting sheep lent added pathos to the cortège. No other voices could be heard; only the weeping of the women as they followed to the field.

The business seemed to fade away. The prosperous farm of Elimelech was left in silence. A pall of grief and gloom hung over the orchards. There were no men. Sadly the days slipped by. They made no plans. The tragedies worked inwardly with Naomi. There seemed no hope. She felt alone, enshrouded in her darkness. It was the end of an era, with no glimmer beyond. 'I am finished now,' she whimpered. 'The hand of the

Lord has gone out against me.' She had buried her husband and buried her boys. 'The Almighty has dealt very bitterly with me.' That is what she believed. Now she would bury her name. She would be called no more Naomi, but Mara, for bitterness.[10]

And what could she do for these Moabite girls?

NOTES

1. Beth Hoglah was a township situated about two miles east of the Jordan and three miles south of Jericho. It means 'a place of magpies' and was situated not far from the estimated location of Beth-abara. It was the scene of John's baptizing; (see Judges 7: 24 and John 1: 28), and speaks, perhaps of a moral decision between 'black' and 'white'. For details of Beth Hoglah and other place names along the borders of Benjamin and Judah, consult Joshua, chapters 15 and 18.
2. Judges 1: 21
3. 'Bohan' was a son of Reuben and could well have been one of the boys who stood surety for Benjamin in Genesis, chapters 42 and 43. This memorial may be linked with that incident. See also, Joshua 18: 17 for this and other associated locations.
4. See Deuteronomy 6: 10–15
5. See Deuteronomy 11: 22–25
6. Naomi spoke of the house of Ruth's mother, (1: 8), an unusual mode of reference, if Ruth's real father were still alive. The father referred to by Boaz, (2: 11), therefore, could be Ruth's stepfather, in which case, Naomi would hesitate to speak of Ruth's family setting in Moab as her father's house. It seems inadequate to suggest that the 'mother's house' was simply the apartment for the women.
7. This conclusion is not the product of contemporary evangelical exposition but goes right back to the Talmud, in which the tragedies befalling the household of Elimelech are viewed as divine retribution for leaving Judah, the appointed inheritance of that tribe. See *Baba Bathra*, 91a.
8. See Deuteronomy 7: 3 and Numbers 25: 1–5 together with Ezra 9: 1–4 by way of illustration. The inclusion of Moabite woman under the heading of 'strange wives' in Ezra's book amounts to an authoritative exposition of Moses by an inspired expert on this point. He also prayed and wept at the tragedy.
9. See Deuteronomy 23: 3. Ellicott in his commentary maintains that the Jewish legal systems viewed this prohibition as applying to the male only, and that Ruth, therefore, would not be touched by this precept. It is the author's opinion, however, that she would have been bound by it, had she not embraced the faith of Jehovah. The identification of the pagan abominations with the pagan wives in Ezra 9: 1–4 seems to support this. Ruth, we must remember, though a Moabitess by birth, became a Jew inwardly, and this surely is what matters (Rom. 2: 29).
10. 'Mara' means 'bitterness'. It looks back to the bitter waters of Exodus 15 that only the tree appointed by the Lord could sweeten. 'Marah' was the name of this oasis, the first station of Israel, east of the Red Sea. 'Mary' is really the same word, a name which was the first utterance of the Risen Christ. In the happy moment of her recognition, all her tears were turned to joy by Him who died upon the Tree.

Eight

Ebb-Tide Turning

> '*God will surely visit you, and ye shall carry up my bones from hence.*'
>
> Genesis 50: 24
>
> '*The Lord had visited His people in giving them bread.*'
>
> Ruth 1: 6
>
> '*the time of thy visitation . . .*'
>
> Luke 19: 44
>
> '*Let us now go even unto Bethlehem, and see this thing which is come to pass . . .*'
>
> Luke 2: 15

THE two main movements of persons in The Book of Ruth are distinguished by the adverbs of time, 'when' and 'then'. '*When* the judges ruled and there was a famine in the land', Elimelech and his family moved out. With deep feeling we have traced the sequel for Naomi. First we read, 'she was left of her two sons'; next we read, 'the woman was left of her two sons and her husband'. It is sorrow upon sorrow and loss upon loss. It is precisely at this stage we notice the second movement and it is signposted by the word 'then'. '*Then*', it says, 'she arose with her daughters-in-law, that she might return . . .' It is in the loss of all we have, so often, that God becomes to us all we need. Just as the narrative indicates an accelerating departure with commensurate loss, so it depicts a progressive exercise of repentance and return, with its consequent blessing. After reading, 'she arose . . . that she might return . . .' we then read, 'she went forth out of the place where she was'. It is followed by further steps in the right direction, 'they went on the way to return unto the land of Judah', until finally we are told, 'they two went until they came to Bethlehem'. The original determination to get out, is first matched and then exceeded by the determination to get back. How reminiscent of the prodigal son, who claimed all his father would give him; who gathered all and took his journey to the far country; and who then spent all and began to be in want. Then it was he came home, only to find, after all, that his all in all was with the Father and in the Father's house. As the Proverbs say, 'Better is a little with the fear of the Lord, than great treasure and trouble therewith'. 'Better is a dinner of herbs where love is, than a stalled ox and hatred therewith.'[1] Better indeed, one crust in the Father's presence than ten thousand dainties in a distant land.

Not only are the histories and teachings of the Bible inspired and therefore true, but the very words in which they are couched are also inspired. 'All Scripture is God breathed', or as it has been translated, 'God breathing'; thus as we read the Scripture and comprehend it, we can say that God breathes out His truth and we breathe it in. One thing we can be sure of, is this, that there is no bad breath with God. 'Every word of God is pure.' We, like Saul of Tarsus, can breath out threatenings and slaughterings, but whether God's breath quickens us or consumes us, it is always clean.

At the time when Ruth was written, there were two terms in current use which described the territories of Israel and Moab respectively. To us this may seem unimportant but such is the accuracy of the very words of Scripture that God has seen to it that these expressions have been preserved and used in their right connotation. The difference in the words did not miss the translators, although in English it is difficult to show the distinction without enlarging the expression. In regard to Israel, we read of it as 'the land'; an area, co-extensive in the Old Testament, with Jehovah's localised and manifest Presence.[2] It was the place in all the earth, where He particularly was. In regard to Moab, however, we read of it as 'the country of Moab'. The difference between these two words is very real. 'The land' refers to a broad expanse of territory and gives more the sense of great horizons and far flung frontiers. The phrase, 'the country' on the other hand, means just a slip of ground, or, if you like, a field.[3] Elimelech and Naomi thus left the wide open spaces of God's inheritance for the paltry patch of seeming plenty in the tiny acres of Moab.

As Naomi now looked on the graves of her loved ones, Moab, to her, had become smaller than ever. All that it offered was summarised there. The way had seemed so right but its end was death. To forsake what God has given, to get what one can without Him, always invites disaster. This hapless family, like many today, fled before physical conditions, rather than search into spiritual reasons. In crisis we always want to do something, whereas God insists that we be something. He is our refuge but we adopt subterfuge. We expect the wrong things in our adversity. We look to Him, but He does not promise to deliver us from it. What He does promise, is to deliver us in it. Safety for the Hebrew children was not in trying to jump out of the fire but in going through the flames with God. 'When thou passest through the fire, He says, "I will be with thee".' Abraham was clearly taught this lesson for even the great in faith are apt to falter on this issue. In all his journeys, he required of Sarah that she pose as his sister. In these false roles, they too left the land and went down into Egypt in fear of a famine. As might have been expected this proved of danger to others and to Abraham's disgrace. He played the same game sometime later, with Abimelech in Gerar, where he almost caused the death of his host and his household. It was only when this deception was confessed that Sarah bore her child. How could God give them Isaac, while such imposture was proceeding. Was God's elect on earth to have a baby by his sister? Let her only be his wife and God would make the barren bear. Neither famine or fertility are problems to Him. The Psalmist crystallises the experience of the believing Israelite when he sings, 'Trust in the Lord and do good; so shalt thou dwell in the land, and verily thou shalt be fed'. The children of believing Abraham, whether in the days of the Judges or in the present days of the Church, should follow not the follies but the faith of the patriarch. Then we, too, shall be God's friends.

As we think of Elimelech in this connection we should remember that to be carnally minded is death and enmity against God, but on the contrary, to be spiritually minded is life and peace. Elimelech had sown to the flesh, and of the flesh, he had reaped corruption. This law is inexorable. 'If ye live after the flesh,' says Paul, 'ye shall die.'[4] Moses, relying on the flesh,

struck an Egyptian and buried him in the sand. At the end of his
days, in an unguarded moment, out came the flesh again. He
struck the rock. Then God buried Moses in the sand. That sand
and cleft of rock was none other than the soil of Moab.[5] This
law is operative in the greatest and the least. In the mouldering
remains of Elimelech and his sons, all this is vocal. It is not only
the witness of Abel that speaks from the ground. Moab looks
back to a cave and leads down to the grave. The name means,
'water of a father'; a sobering thought. For whether our father
be the devil, fallen Adam, or failing Lot; as our father is, so shall
we be. Sodom's immorality was Moab's beginning.[6] Sodom's
fate will be his end, for Zephaniah writes in his prophecy,
'Surely Moab shall be as Sodom and the children of Ammon
(Moab's brother) as Gomorrah, even the breeding of nettles, and
saltpits, and a perpetual desolation . . . this shall they have for
their pride, because they have reproached and magnified themselves against the people of the Lord of Hosts.'[7] So 'the flesh
lusts against the Spirit and the Spirit against the flesh'. Now
Naomi is as vexed as Lot, and even more so. O to escape the web
of sorrows that Moab weaves! Naomi has reached the end. She
will arise and go.

Her change of heart immediately affects her vision. It heals it.
The rose-coloured spectacles of faithless sight are utterly discarded. That grass beyond the hedge which seemed so sweet, is
spine-filled cactus now. The famine in Bethlehem is remembered
as fulness, and Moab's plenty collapses in emptiness. This is an
evaluation and is soon followed by an evacuation, but the text
makes plain that both resulted from 'evangelisation'. Her
readiness to return to the Lord, was occasioned by a word from
the Lord. 'She arose that she might return,' it says, 'for she had
heard in the country[8] of Moab, how that the Lord had visited
His people in giving them bread.' This was good news indeed.
What is strange, however, is that it only registered now. There
can be little doubt that Israel's recovery and renewed prosperity
had been common knowledge for quite a while. In all proba-
bility at this time, there was adequate food for all in both Moab
and Israel. What made the difference was that the bearer of the
good news expounded the fact of bread in Bethlehem as a
visitation of Jehovah. Thus economic intelligence became a

spiritual revelation. Many people know the facts of how Jesus was born at Bethlehem and find them food for thought, but it is only when they see in Jesus, God Himself incarnate, that the concept of a divine visitation creates within them obeisance and obedience. Naomi's informant remains unnamed. He did not proclaim himself, but only what the Lord had wrought. As Paul puts it, 'We preach not ourselves but Jesus Christ . . .' He represents the true evangelist. She heard his news and turned to God, even as one day, when the Baptist spoke men heard his word and followed Jesus. How good to be unknown, when well known, but this can only be if our praise is in the Gospel.[9]

The more Naomi dwelt upon these tidings, the more she was enlightened by the Lord. Everything began to fall into place. In Bethlehem, it was not only a time of grain but a time of grace. God was good. He was in their food. This temporal blessing meant spiritual favour. The famine and its cause was more and more apparent. The Lord had been affronted by the evil of His people. She had not viewed herself, before, as one of the transgressors, but simply a victim of circumstance; and what a victim, she might say, if mere self-pity could relieve her wounds. It is interesting to note that the good tidings found her just where she was, and came when needed most. She had been as the epistle puts it, 'foolish, disobedient, deceived, serving different lusts and pleasures . . . but . . . the kindness and love of God, the Saviour appeared.'[10] The Lord who had broken the whole staff of bread by reason of their sin had now appeared in salvation at Bethlehem, visiting His people and answering their cry. She would go again to Bethlehem. That was her place. Where she was and where the word had found her, only emphasised her wrong position and her sad condition. She was convicted. She could stay no longer. The Moabites' father was not her father and their gods were not her gods. Where they dwelt was no place for her. She was an Israelite. Before it had been in name only, now she would be one with all her heart.

Centuries later, Jeremiah sketched the profile of the Moabite people. 'Moab', he said, 'hath been at ease from his youth, and he hath settled on his lees and hath not been emptied from vessel to vessel.'[11] If the source of Moab was lust, then the course of Moab was laziness. It speaks of the line of least resistance; of feeding on the labours of others, of exploiting the weak; of getting without giving; a life, born out of indulgence, and boasting in indolence. Moab had appealed to Elimelech and Naomi, precisely along these lines. It was the easy way out but proved as we have seen, the quickest way down. Moab then, is the flesh in preponderance and the world on its way. Balak in his treachery, Eglon in his greed and Mesha in his rebellion,[12] these three kings of Moab, sum up its character. They were of their father the devil and his works did they do. They flourished in their wickedness like the green bay tree. For much of their history they were not troubled as other men. Like many a sinner, they seemed to live, for the most part a 'charmed' life. Moab is not emptied, necessarily, from vessel to vessel. He goes on heedless to his end in Sodomite indifference. The professing believer, however, who, like Naomi, tries to make the best of both worlds comes under discipline. If we try to keep a small stake in God's inheritance yet meanwhile feast on Moab's fatness, we are asking to be emptied. The world may do what it likes! It seems to get away with it, but not so the believer. Moab may not be emptied but Naomi is. 'I went out full,' she says, 'but the Lord has brought me home again empty.' The effect of the Lord's visitation is to bring her to this confession. In this she is sincere. She does not blame Elimelech, but herself alone. '*I* have sinned,' is the true sign of the repentant prodigal. No doubt she remembered how she had pestered her husband and swayed his judgment; how she had appealed to his tenderness and suggested their leaving. Whatever blame attached to Elimelech and no doubt there was plenty, for he was her head, she does not raise it.[13] 'I went out,' she says, 'and I went out full.' Maybe I had little to eat in Israel, but I had everything to make me happy had I but known it. Now she had been emptied from vessel to vessel, and what remained? Nothing to go home with but a broken spirit and a contrite heart. In this though, she was richer than she had ever been. Circumstance had caught her but consequence had taught her. She was growing in her experience of God. Her departure was her undoing, but her return was all His doing. 'The Lord brought me home,' she says. But how did He do it? She recites a catalogue of woes. At first it smacks of recrimination, but whatever anguish of soul is here revealed, her statement shows an ever deepening perception of God's chastening. At first she is more conscious of His severity, but increasingly of His goodness, and in the end of His kindness.

> '*The hand of the Lord is gone out against me,*' *she says* (1 : 13).
> '*The Almighty has dealt very bitterly with me*' (1 : 20).
> '*The Lord hath testified against me*' (1 : 21).
> '*The Almighty hath afflicted me*' (1 : 21).

Though left of her husband and left of her sons, she is not left of the Lord. She has actually been left alive, and that for a purpose. He has been coming to her in two ways; as Jehovah, that is as *Lord* of the Covenant; and secondly, as the *Almighty*, that is as Shaddai, the God of Abraham. In view of the Sinai covenant, He is emphasising His Lordship and how she is morally responsible to Him. She belongs to that chosen race, who declared that all He said, they would do. As the God of Abraham, he was emphasising how He was morally responsible for her. He was committed to her and her people, in all His promises concerning their seed and the land. That he had dealings with her should banish despair and inspire fresh wonder and confidence. He had not dropped her. He was going on with her. He had not removed her but preserved her. In all these ways He was bringing her home. His hand may hurt her but it also held her. He may chastise her but it brought Him near. Later she says, 'He hath not left off His kindness . . .' It was the sweet recognition of the unfailing faithfulness of God to one His love would not forsake.

NOTES

1. Proverbs 15 : 16–17
2. See II Kings 24 : 20 and Jeremiah 52 : 3
3. For the use of this word elsewhere in Scripture and evidence of its restricted sense, see I Samuel 6 : 1 and Obadiah 19.
4. See Romans 8 and Galatians 6
5. Deuteronomy 34 : 5–6
6. See Genesis 19 : 30–38
7. Zephaniah 2 : 9. Lot escaped the fate of Sodom but his ultimate posterity must share it.
8. The word 'country' meaning 'a field', is in the plural (1 : 1) when Naomi goes to the 'country of Moab'. But when she leaves it (1 : 6), the word

is in the singular. The world looks so great when we seek it, but it is as nothing once we taste its bitter fruit.

9. II Corinthians 8 : 18
10. Titus 3 : 3-4
11. Jeremiah 48 : 11
12. II Kings 3 : 5-7
13. It is worth noting that the Scripture does not actually employ the expression, 'the man is the head of the house'. In I Timothy 3 : 4, 5, 12, where he is spoken of as ruling his house the word seems to emphasise not so much the strong arm of government, that is 'force', but his standing before his house as its appointed leader for the word is 'proistēmi', 'to place over or before'. This rules out the thought of a man domineering his family and brandishing the aforementioned cliché as an authority for over-riding their wishes whatever they may be. The implication of the word employed to describe his rule, is, that by moral example and spiritual guidance, he is to lead his family through the years as they face the experiences of life together. The wife and the children will look to him, not because he demands respect but because he commands it as he stands and goes before them in uprightness, compassion, and dependability. The Scripture does say, however, that 'he is head of the woman' (1 Cor : 11). The woman's activities in the home and the handling of its affairs are to be carried out, therefore, under, and in the exercise of the authority of her husband, as he leads the family under the authority of Christ. 'The heart of her husband is to safely trust in her.' It is in the recognition of her head, that the woman is liberated. She is then what I Timothy 5 : 14, describes as, the 'oiko-despotēs'. This is a powerful expression, for it literally means, the 'household despot' and thus the guide of the household affairs in no uncertain terms. In the degree that a woman honours her Christ-controlled husband, she implements in her control of the children and her household management, the divine authority of Christ invested in him. It thus becomes obligatory for children to obey their parents in the Lord. This spiritual supervision of the family is the touchstone of spiritual effectiveness in the local church (I Timothy 3 : 5). If however, the woman ceases to guide the house along these lines and begins to goad her husband along her own lines; if she usurps his headship and dominates him either in secret, before the children or even in public, then she is beginning to destroy the very thing God ordained her to preserve.

Nine

The Great Divide

> *'Choose you this day whom ye will serve; whether the gods which your fathers served . . . or the gods of the Amorites . . .: but as for me and my house, we will serve the Lord.'*
>
> Joshua 24: 15
>
> *'And they called Rebekah, and said unto her, "Wilt thou go . . .?" And she said, "I will go".'*
>
> Genesis 24: 58
>
> *'And Ruth said, "Intreat me not to leave thee, or to return from following after thee; for whither thou goest, I will go . . ." '*
>
> Ruth 1: 16

THROUGH the long empty days, the sad, soulful eyes of the three widows looked out, as to a vacant universe. The days wore on. The world went by. The visitors grew less. Their grief that moved so many in the days of death, moved folk no longer. They nursed their broken hearts alone. Ruth sat for hours, numbed and subdued. Orpah burned incense to her idols. Naomi worked on, attending to the household chores. The farm was no more viable. Few things were really saleable. It seemed that all was in suspense, yet things were happening. The news from Bethlehem had come. The smoking flax of Naomi's faith fanned to a flame. Ruth, amenable from youth toward the God of the patriarchs, though hardly knowing who He was, found her heart warming, as Naomi told her of her hearth and home. Since she had known the family, they had spoken little of their birthplace and even less of God, but tragedy is a sure instructor and life's rebukes are wisdom to the attentive ear. There was a change in her mother-in-law, a softening of the face, as if some Lover, quite unseen, had come to fill her aching heart. The two would often sit, talking on into the twilight. Orpah, too, sometimes drew near. Could the God of the hills be a god for the valleys? She did not know, nor dare she ponder. From the farmstead, in fair weather, it was possible to see the skyline of the hills of Judah. They never seemed to look the same. Sunshine and shadow gave them mood. Naomi felt a love returning; a wondering at His visitation, a reflection growing to conviction; a willingness to plan and go.

Eventually there came the day when she opened her heart to her daughters in law. She had trembled at this. It went against her natural affections, especially at this time of sorrow. They had grown much closer in their mutual grief. The differences of age and race seemed nothing now. How could she leave them? Their reaction came, at first, as a glad surprise. They would come too, they told her. If she had come to them in the valley, could they not go with her to the mountains. Their lives over many a year had been woven together. Should the strands be now unravelled. They had been of comfort to each other in the days of affliction. Why not also in the days to come?

Whilst Naomi had her second thoughts, she said no more. Could two sad, lonely girls from Moab, find any place in her society. It seemed unlikely. Slowly the business was concluded. The proceeds of the farm were not so great. Once people in the surrounding hamlets knew of their impending move, they would not offer half the price. Naomi's conscience, too, was tender. They never bought it in the first place. They stood in dead men's shoes and tilled in dead men's ground. Ten years had passed and now her own loved men were dead. What money could she take from Moab? The expense of three quick funerals had whittled down their ready cash, and once outstanding debts were paid, the balance due to each proved, after all, quite small . . . .

At last the day to leave was with them. It touched her much to see the girls. Where did they think their future lay? It remained to be seen what they would do. The banks of Jordan would reveal it. Few friends escorted them on the road to the west. Ruth and Orpah had seen but little of their people since marrying into the Hebrew family. The in-laws never really mixed. Ruth's mother showed small interest in her daughter, though Orpah visited her folk sometimes. How strong the links would prove, was difficult for Naomi to know. She felt concerned at pulling them away. She had not asked them to go with her. It was their own idea. Now it was trying as the time drew near, to really pose the problems to them. They were her only links with Mahlon and Chilion. She loved them dearly and valued their company, yet felt unable to lead them to Bethlehem and to the worship of God.

The fords of Jordan brought back memories for Ruth. No one could know, not even Naomi, what it meant for her at the river that night. It all came back so vividly, as if it were yesterday. Before retiring to the inn, she stood alone and looked across the water in the silver moonlight. She thought of her mother on that dreadful day when her father was murdered; of the young guard at her bedside; and the helter-skelter all the way to the river. As she relived those terror filled moments, her eyes became more aware of the landscape. She picked out the ruins on the mound of Jericho. They seemed to rise amidst the moonbeams, till her father's fortress, grotesque and pitiless, took shape again. She remembered its outline, still all so familiar. Reality merged with the threads of her fantasy. She was there in her wistfulness, up on the battlements. How drawn she had been, that night, to those everlasting hills! How lost in their mystery under the stars! The same deep sense of wonder swept through her now, as if she were caught up into something she could not understand, something exceedingly great and so very splendid. Amongst the twinkling lights of heaven, one star seemed brighter than them all. It drew her eyes, until her dark black pupils glistened with its radiant splendour. What was it Balaam said, the words of their soothsayer?

> *'there shall come a Star out of Jacob,*
> *and a Sceptre shall rise out of Israel,*
> *and shall smite the corners of Moab,*
> *and destroy all the children of Sheth . . .*
> > *Israel shall do valiantly.*
> > *Out of Jacob shall come He*
> > *That shall have the dominion . . .'*[1]

She looked straight before her, for what seemed a long time. 'There is no hope for Moab,' she said to herself, 'there is no hope'. She had felt that way for years. She knew it now. The light of her star lit a path across Jordan. 'It is the way to Bethlehem!' she exclaimed. And suddenly the banks of the river were more than a political boundary. They were the frontiers of destiny and the end of despair.

NOTES

1. Numbers 24 : 17

Ten

The Place of Many Waters

'Whom have I in heaven but Thee? and there is none upon earth that I desire beside Thee. My flesh and my heart faileth: but God is the strength of my heart, and my portion for ever.'

Psalm 73: 25, 26

'Lord, to whom shall we go . . . ?'

John 6: 68

THE next morning, very early, the three women were astir. Arrows of brilliant sunshine shot through the latticed windows, as if to say, The day is victor. Arise! March westward with the light! They looked towards the crossing. The swirling waters of the Jordan, opaque and yellow, were running high, for Jordan overflows its banks in harvest. Well in, along the jetty, was moored a rough pontoon, shifting uneasily, as if tugging to be free. Two doubtful looking characters, who plied its trade and superintended its inflated ox-skins, were dangling their nets in the river, presumably to catch some breakfast. And not too far away, some enterprising housewife was thrashing sodden clothes upon a big round stone. With the night scene still so fresh in her mind, Ruth looked eagerly at the broad expanse of water. The hills of Moab, at her back, projected strong, harsh shadows across the threshold of the promised land. The ragged skeleton of her father's fortress gaped uncouthly at the dawn. But soon the sun was up. The symbols and their fears were broken. This was a day of new beginnings. The things of night would cloud her hopes no more.

As they gathered their baggage together, they spoke little to each other. Each packed their personal things into their own skin-pouches and shouldered them to the river, where the ferry was awaiting them. There is loneliness in decision. It was, of course, supposed to have been made, yet each, in their own way, knew there was more to be said and something yet to be done. Decisions are only real, when implemented, and they had come to such a moment now.

Naomi prepared to go on board. Once she reached the boat-men, the haggling for the fare would start; but prior to that, the price of leaving must be weighed. Suddenly she turned, and her soft dark eyes, mellowed by suffering, searched the inner-most depths of the Moabite women. She lifted her arms and em-braced each of her daughters-in-law in turn. She did so with a moving tenderness, catching her breath and biting her lips, lest tears should flow. Her face flushed with emotion. 'I think you should go back now,' she said, softly, hardly able to express the words. 'Your mothers will so look for you.' The sorrows of the past seemed, all at once, to mount like pent up waters, in their faces. They had been through everything together. 'It is where you belong,' said Naomi, 'back there in your old homes, isn't it? Where you were brought up. All your friends are there.'

But Ruth felt she had no friends; and that she had no home where she had been brought up. As Naomi clasped her again, Ruth found herself looking out across her shoulder at that 'old mausoleum'. Her childhood languished there in the long hot summers. What a monument to her father! A coarse, crude emblem of a gutted life. She thought again of her grey-haired mother, and how, on that unforgettable day, they had ridden up her favourite valley, with everything so sad and everything so beautiful; and how the river had run red in the sunset with the blood of the slain. Strange how her mother should lose her husband in Israel, and her mother-in-law should lose her husband in Moab. For a brief moment, Elimelech came before her. He had been quite bewildered when he came, Mahlon had told her; partly because of the change of scene but also as a reaction from the harsh privations her own cruel father had inflicted. Yet, how princely Elimelech had acted, compared to the implacable Eglon. She never saw her father in his hour of death. Only her mother spoke of that blood. But she did see Elimelech. He had known the True God once. He died a broken man with-out Him. Her own father had been a devotee of Chemosh,[1] a slave to the fire-god and the star of ill-omen. How often he had gone to Dibon and its temple, away north of the Arnon. What stories she had overheard, as the guards had whispered of his vile obscenities and the devilish rites he had performed. But suddenly his star had fallen and now the Star of Jacob shone. The God of Elimelech was king; of this she was sure.

As Naomi held her still, Ruth's head drooped slowly downwards. The warmth and nearness of the older woman infused a comfort which she could not measure. She gazed intently at the stones and sand. It was her Moabite soil she saw, and the thought of it moved her. It took her to her husband's grave. Just twelve short months ago, they had buried him; in ground the very same as this, back there on the farm at the foot of the dunes. The cactus, she remembered, was a riot of colour; such thorny magnificence! Its blooms were dead next day. Flowers, like loved ones, hardly linger. They quickly pass away. Her marriage, she felt, had been a sad one. Not that Mahlon had been unkind. In fact it was his mildness that she had loved.[2] He had been so different from her father. But he had never been robust; not really. Naomi had told her that. There had been no children to gladden her with laughter. She had never held a baby in her arms. There had been no 'fluttering of those far off wings . . .' All passed before her as a dream. The scene about her was ethereal; the air so still. Only the waters flowing, told her of passing things. In that sequestered moment, it seemed that time itself stood still.

Once again she looked at Naomi. Her eyes were red, her cheeks like fire. She also had her turmoil, though born of different reasons. She sensed her suffering. Poor Naomi! How well she knew her now. She was blaming herself for their heartaches and their sorrows. She was telling herself she should never have left Bethlehem, and transmitted her woes. Yet in her mother in law, Ruth saw a nobility. Her faith though weak, had never been abandoned. She despised the Moabite images. Chemosh had always been anathema; a thorn in her side and a sword in her bones. Ruth knew that this returning was no mere longing for her native land, but a going back to Him, whom she had slighted, yet somehow still believed. Ruth felt the deep realities that charged the moment, yet standing there between two worlds, she seemed so very far away. Grief isolates; so does

the immortal choice. Beyond the ageing figure of the one she
loved, Ruth glimpsed again, the timeless hills; beyond those
furrowed features, the riven mountains of her God. They rose in
their immensity. O unimagined Strength! Upward and higher,
still she looked, till all the land was her horizon. To whom
should she go if not to Jehovah? And whom should she trust
if not the Almighty? 'O God of Abraham!' her heart was
crying, 'Thou God of Isaac and of Israel! Thou God of all my
yesterdays, be *my* God from today!'

So completely absorbed was Ruth in her own deep musings,
she barely realised that Naomi had gone on speaking. 'The
Lord be kind³ to you both,' she was saying, 'for you have been
so kind to my boys.' The words fell sadly from her quivering
lips. 'And what can I say of your kindness to me? The Lord
watch over you, and if it please Him, give you fresh husbands,
and rest in their care.' Then she kissed them both, as if she had
borne them. The tragic words and touch of lips released the
floodgates of their tears. Uncontrollably they wept, till fellow-
passengers and bystanders felt surely they must turn their gaze.
There is a solitude in grief, that tends to stop another's stare. A
sense of apprehension gripped Ruth's heart. The way over
Jordan was worse than she thought.

'But we will come with you, Naomi,' they pleaded. 'Yes, all
the way to Bethlehem and be your daughters there.' It was
moving to Naomi to hear their avowals, but who was she to urge
them on. Her mind reverted to the natural. They must take
stock. Their need as women, let them face it, was for husbands.
Her years were passing. She saw them destitute and undefended.
She had no positive solution. 'It is not practical,' she argued.
'Think sensibly. What can I offer you. I'm now too old to be of
use. Why, if tonight I could conceive, you could not wait for
sons of mine. The thing's impossible. My Mahlon and my
Chilion died. I feel somehow I lost them for you. The Lord's
hand is against me. There is no more that I can do. Why will
you go with me? Your past was scarred through being with me.
Your future you should seek back home.'

She did not mean to be unkind, or wrongly counsel good
intention. It was her mood of self-effacement. Backslider, as
she was, she felt incompetent to call out faith. She was suggest-

ing in effect, 'There is only one thing for you to do as far as I am concerned, and that is, to go back to the point where we first met, and start again. All I can say is, the Lord be merciful to you and treat you both as you have treated me. I can make no further contribution to your life of happiness. My witness is finished. Now I must cut my losses, get out of the place of my humiliation, and back to the place where I first left the road.' That she should make these proposals exposes her impotence. That God uses her questions, shows His omnipotence. God searches motives and the hearts intent. He may not condone what we say, but, nonetheless, can superintend its impact on the folk who hear it. Discipleship is always searched by Jesus. He also saw two following, and asked, 'What seek ye?' Their answer proved most precious in His sight. 'Master, where dwellest Thou?' they asked. In this their hearts were manifest. What He desired for them was what they dared to ask of Him. They would be with Him where He was. They wanted not so much the place, but Christ, Himself, the Living Person. Christ would be loved, not for His mansions but Himself alone. Why will ye go with me? asks Naomi in all her inward desolation. It is her question, but God is in the question too. He knows their answers and their secrets. The girls must state them now or never. It is His testing at the river. Her heart must first be bared, whose hand would take the plough with God.

As Naomi rebuffs their hopes, she sees herself their biggest disappointment. The girls dissolve again to tears. They weep convulsively, their whole frame heaving. The boatmen wait in some annoyance. The minutes pass. Conclusion loiters. Then Orpah moves. She gives to Naomi just one more kiss, then slips her arms. She takes, with hesitance, a slow step backwards, her hands still lightly clasping Naomi's. One more step back. She lets them fall. The act is simple. The effect is binding.[4] The sense of disengagement heightens. It is the severing of a contact. She speaks her last appreciation, then gives the gesture of farewell. They see her turn. She lifts her things and walks away. They watch her shrinking figure moving eastwards into Moab. She does not look to them again. So 'Naomi grieves as Orpah leaves'. Thank God! 'Ruth cleaves!'

But we should remember that Orpah's name means, 'youth-

ful'.[5] It speaks of immaturity. Hers was an uncompleted exercise;
a movement in the soul that left the spirit still unquickened; a
gesture of intent that baulked at action. 'I go, sir,' said the
child, but never went. Our Master tells the story. He also talks
of seed received, which took no root. Accepted with joy it wilted
when tested. The Adamic bedrock was not broken. It never
brought forth fruit for God. What the story of Orpah tells us is
that emotion is not to be confused with devotion. Emotion, if
evoked by circumstance, changes with changing scenes. Devotion is different. As the fruit of conviction, it ripens in all winds
and weathers. Orpah had emotion but she did not have devotion.
Ruth also had emotion but it was not primary. Her treasure was
a devotion, rooted not even in affection, though that was there,
but in conviction. It is not how we feel about someone that
changes our relationship. It is through leaving and cleaving we
are joined to another. When we act on conviction, we make our
decision because the step is the *right* one, then affections and
emotions all take their place.

As Orpah passes from the page of history, Naomi turns to
Ruth and states the meaning of her choice. 'Your sister-in-law
has gone back to her people.' That is to say, 'blood is thicker
than water'. The natural was strong. She was finally a Moabite.
But she also adds most significantly, 'and to her gods'. The
satanically spiritual, proved stronger still. The bonds of sentiment were quite unequal to the thraldom of devilry. Chemosh
and his minions kept their prey. Orpah retreats to the scene of
her tragedy. A little while, and she is lost in antiquity. Death she
has known. The second death will be her portion. From the
fringe of light she goes back to the darkness. This is the condemnation.[6]

Like myriads of others, it was *her* choice. There is no blame
with heaven.

Naomi's arm lifts in the folds of her garment and points after
Orpah. 'She has gone,' she says. Then turning to Ruth she
declares, 'And surely it is time for you.' Overshadowed by her
own stark failure, she seeks a settlement that will leave her to
her grief alone. She does not really assess what she is doing. It
is enough. It has all been so harrowing. She wants to close the
chapter. How can she cope with Ruth? She is saying in her

frantic weakness, Let us say no more. Let me go my way and
you go yours. But this, of course, is never good enough for God.
Nor was it good enough for Ruth. To a person less convinced
of her course, such words might well have been disastrous.
Because we handle things awry, we cannot quietly slip away,
or call for premature foreclosure. Our faithlessness must not
deny that others have the faith we lack. Because we falter, it is
no reason to conclude that others have no moral stamina. Where
we have failed, they can endure. Once down, how hard it is for
us to see above our own small stature. God does not sanction
Naomi's word, but lets it be His final probe to bring Ruth's
trust in Him to focus. 'And will ye also go', says Jesus to the
twelve. Christ's question drew from Simon Peter the noblest
personal recognition. So here, once challenged, Ruth responds.
Her name means 'friendship'. Her faith proclaims that doubly
true. The words she spoke remain untarnished. Breathing
reality, they last for eternity. The arms of Chemosh close on
Orpah; God's everlasting arms reach out to Ruth.

> *'Intreat me not to leave thee,' she says,*
> *'or to return from following after thee:*
> *for whither thou goest, I will go:*
> *and where thou lodgest, I will lodge:*
> *thy people shall be my people*
> *and thy God, my God:*
> *Where thou diest, will I die,*
> *and there will I be buried:*
> *the Lord do so to me, and more also,*
> *if ought but death part thee and me.'*

This marriage to the will of God has been beautifully summarised :
   'She found a new path for her feet; a new place for her home:
a new people for her friends; a new power for her life; a new
prospect for her future.'[7] Or to put it in other words with the
emphasis on the progressive steps of her confession: Hers was
a new direction, bringing her to a new habitation; introducing
her to a new generation and giving her a new adoration. In life
and in death she had a new expectation and a new aspiration.
All this is very wonderful and undoubtedly inspired; but notice,

too, the intensity of her commital for she embarks upon an invocation of the Lord to maintain her in her new allegiance. It is a strong expression and is used by Eli in adjuring Samuel to tell him the truth. It is used by Jonathan in his pledge to David. It is used by David, himself, in his vow against Nabal; but this expression of such serious moment and far reaching consequence is found first on the lips of Ruth.[8] Real faith and real dedication always find their expression. Whatever the cost, she is going through. Out of the abundance of her heart, she speaks.

After this we read, 'When Naomi saw she was steadfastly minded to go with her, then she left speaking unto her.' This sentence pinpoints the wellspring of Ruth's memorable choice, 'a steadfast mind'. It is the Hebrew 'amats' and in the context, infers that she strengthened herself to go. This is the same word that God uses when He exhorts Joshua to be of good courage. It could mean to make oneself hard, that is 'to steel oneself' against disuasion; to be impervious to all proposals that would weaken resolve. But the word is also used in the Psalms,[9] where we are enjoined to 'wait on the Lord; be of good courage (a different word), and He shall strengthen thine heart.' The Hebrew 'amats' is the basis of the last phrase here and refers in this case, to *God* strengthening our hearts. 'Naomi was a back-slider coming home. Ruth was an outsider coming in.' Both had made their decisions. In this sense they had the courage of their convictions. They had strengthened themselves to act in the light they had. But when at last they reached Bethlehem, Naomi says, 'The Lord brought me home' and we can be sure, that Ruth's testimony would ever be, 'The Lord brought me in'. We are responsible to believe and to be strong in faith, giving glory to God. There is no doubt about the reality of faith, but faith can only be strong, when rooted in the grace of the God who saves. His strength is ministered to us in our infirmity. When in utter weakness our faith, born of His Word, lays hold on His promises, we become strong in the Lord and the power of His might. So He strengthens, as He says to us, 'Be strong!'

The struggling women step on board and the boatmen cast off from the jetty. The mountains of Moab grow fainter. The hills of the Lord draw nearer. Their movement is acclaimed in heaven. A few more minutes and they disembark. Old things

are passed away. The new things beckon. It is the overcoming
way.

NOTES

1. Chemosh was the national deity of the Moabites and the Ammonites,
   a brazen image whose arms enclosed the sacrificial fire. Jerome identifies
   this god with Baal-peor. Elsewhere, Chemosh is declared to be Baalzebub
   and others equate his idols with Mars, or Saturn, the star of ill-omen.
   The Moabites were called 'the people of Chemosh' (Numbers 21:19),
   and Chemosh, 'the god of the Moabites' (II Kings 11:33). The nation
   and its gods are thus viewed in Scripture as being totally identified one
   with the other. It was *their* abomination (II Kings 23:13).
2. Coates views Mahlon's name, which also means 'mildness', as indicative
   of his disposition.
3. 'The Lord deal faithfully in love with you' is apparently the force of the
   words employed. It is a strong expression which 'kindness' quite in-
   adequately conveys.
4. She let go at the point of spiritual decision. The physical does affect the
   spiritual. For instance, the rising from one's knees at a certain point in
   prayer may well mean the turning of faith from pursuing its goal. Ruth
   however 'clings' and in 'clinging' prevails.
5. It also means 'neck'. Perhaps she was high-necked from birth, a certain
   concept of beauty; but she proved 'stiff-necked', that is stubborn, at the
   last.
6. See John 3:19
7. *Twelve Hundred Notes, Quotes and Anecdotes* by A. Naismith, M.A.
8. 'The Lord do so to me, and more also . . .' This mode of invocation is
   used by God's servants as follows: by Ruth in 1:17; by Eli in I Samuel
   3:17; by Jonathan in I Samuel 20:13; by David in I Samuel 25:22. It
   is also used by the ungodly. By Saul in I Samuel 14:44; by Jezebel in
   I Kings 19:2; be Benhadad in I Kings 20:10; and II Kings 6:31.
9. Psalms 27:14

A DAY IN THE FIELDS OF BOAZ

THE FIRST OF THE BARLEY
FIELD OF FAVOUR
THE IDENTIFICATION
UNDER HIS WINGS
HANDFULS OF PURPOSE

So they two went until they came to Bethlehem. And it came to pass, when they were come to Bethlehem, that all the city was moved about them, and they said, Is this Naomi?

And she said unto them, Call me not Naomi, call me Mara: for the Almighty hath dealt very bitterly with me.

I went out full, and the Lord hath brought me home again empty: why then call ye me Naomi, seeing the Lord hath testified against me, and the Almighty hath afflicted me?

So Naomi returned, and Ruth the Moabitess, her daughter in law, with her, which returned out of the country of Moab: and they came to Bethlehem in the beginning of barley harvest.

And Naomi had a kinsman of her husband's, a mighty man of wealth, of the family of Elimelech; and his name was Boaz.

And Ruth the Moabitess said unto Naomi, Let me now go to the field, and glean ears of corn after him in whose sight I shall find grace. And she said unto her, Go, my daughter.

And she went, and came, and gleaned in the field after the reapers: and her hap was to light on a part of the field belonging unto Boaz, who was of the kindred of Elimelech.

And, behold, Boaz came from Bethlehem, and said unto the reapers, The Lord be with you. And they answered him, The Lord bless thee.

Then said Boaz unto his servant that was set over the reapers, Whose damsel is this?

And the servant that was set over the reapers answered and said, It is the Moabitish damsel that came back with Naomi out of the country of Moab:

And she said, I pray you, let me glean and gather after the reapers among the sheaves: so she came, and hath continued even from the morning until now, that she tarried a little in the house.

Then said Boaz unto Ruth, Hearest thou not, my daughter? Go not to glean in another field, neither go from hence, but abide here fast by my maidens.

Let thine eyes be on the field that they do reap, and go thou after them: have I not charged the young men that they shall not touch thee? and when thou art athirst, go unto the vessels, and drink of that which the young men have drawn.

Then she fell on her face, and bowed herself to the ground, and said unto him, Why have I found grace in thine eyes, that thou shouldest take knowledge of me, seeing I am a stranger?

And Boaz answered and said unto her, It hath fully been shewed me, all that thou hast done unto thy mother in law since the death of thine husband: and how thou hast left thy father and thy mother, and the land of thy nativity, and art come unto a people which thou knewest not heretofore.

The Lord recompense thy work, and a full reward be given thee of the Lord God of Israel, under whose wings thou art come to trust.

Then she said, Let me find favour in thy sight, my lord; for that thou hast comforted me, and for that thou hast spoken friendly unto thine handmaid, though I be not like unto one of thine handmaidens.

And Boaz said unto her, At mealtime come thou hither, and eat of the bread, and dip thy morsel in the vinegar. And she sat beside the reapers: and he reached her parched corn, and she did eat, and was sufficed, and left.

And when she was risen up to glean, Boaz commanded his young men, saying, Let her glean even among the sheaves, and reproach her not:

And let fall also some of the handfuls of purpose for her, and leave them, that she may glean them, and rebuke her not.

So he gleaned in the field until even, and beat out that she had gleaned: and it was about an ephah of barley.

Eleven

The First of the Barley

> 'The Lord thy God bringeth thee into a good land, a
> land of brooks of water, of fountains and depths that
> spring out of valleys and hills; a land of wheat, and
> barley . . .'
>
> Deuteronomy 8: 7, 8
>
> 'I will say to the reapers . . . gather the wheat into
> my barn.'
>
> Matthew 13: 30

As the two women stepped from the boat in the humid atmosphere of the Jordan valley, high up on the hills at Bethlehem,
Boaz, son of Salmon, stood with his chief steward in the family
courtyard, discussing the arrangements for the barley harvest.[1]
The hour was early and the air was keen. Servants passed to and
fro across the flagstones. Water was being carried into the house.
A girl fetched eggs for the cook; and as each passed, they spoke
a greeting to their master, who acknowledged their 'shalom'.[2]

'I was out yesterday,' Boaz was saying. 'and I think the main
field is just about ready.'

'I agree, sir,' replied the steward, 'but on the lower side,
where the grain doesn't get the sun so long, I think it could do
a day or two yet.'

'May be you're right. Perhaps you should start this year, as
high up the slope as you can, then by the time you get round to
where you're talking about, it will be ripe enough to cut. But
I think we should get going today. The weather is perfect, and
we need every good day we can get. You know, yourself, it's not
impossible to get a spell of rain, or even snow in harvest.'[3] The
steward looked incredulously at his master.

'I don't remember any since I've been here,' he said. 'Still,
a bite in the air could keep the laggards moving. There's always
a few.'

'I hold you responsible for that,' retorted Boaz, with a smile. 'I pay you, remember, to hire the right people!'

'Well we've got a good bunch this year.'

'Get going, then!' ordered Boaz, 'I'll be back in half an hour to have a look at them.'

The steward left to round up the locals he had hired and Boaz went indoors to get his breakfast. Down through the streets and alleys of Bethlehem, the shouts of the would-be reapers rang from house to house, and soon, a ragged stream of men, women and children were wending their way to the courtyard. Many of them were still in their teens. Most of the older ones were women of the poorer classes, probably widows; but there were also some quite young mothers, eager to add to their family store. Their labour, though, was of doubtful worth, what with the youngsters trailing behind, and grasping their skirts.

Boaz viewed the assembled company with good humour. Harvest was really a festive time and he was not in the habit of making his first briefing too intense. He motioned the steward to start speaking. The steward was a faithful man, who, by his appointment from Boaz, superintended the entire harvest.[4] He gave each worker his task, and maintained good order in the field. He understood what Boaz wanted, and interpreted his every directive in understandable terms to the peasantry at his command. As the steward spoke, Boaz stood behind him, his piercing, yet compassionate eyes scrutinising every person who would reap in his fields. Their conduct greatly concerned him. He knew from experience, that by the time the seven or eight weeks were finished (and it took that to reap both the wheat and the barley), some of the women grew tired. This meant that the children got into mischief or even into danger. Parents must act responsibly to the end. Then the young folk, thrown into close proximity through the daily work and the communal feeding, grew more permissive as the weeks went by, unless a rigorous watch on discipline were kept. The code and conduct of the harvest field was heard by all with dutiful submission. They were just like children waiting resignedly, until the parent's lecture was over, so they could run off and do what they liked. Once the session was finished, the equipment was issued from the barn and everybody trooped out to the fields, sickles and forks aloft, singing as they went.

The path they took straggled out of town between low walls composed of stones, long since culled from the soil either side. Here and there, adjacent to the more wealthy homes, grew groves of olive trees, but even so, a bare half mile still brought them to the open spaces. The barley looked magnificent, like a carpet with a pale gold pile, set in an apartment of blue and surrounded by a wainscot of hills. As they walked along, one of the labourers paused a moment to comment on an over-grown stretch, which stood incongruously amidst the ripening grain.

'Whose field is that?' he asked a neighbour.

'I don't know,' came the answer. 'Strange, though, how nothing's growing in it.'

'O there's plenty growing in it,' he replied. 'Just look at the thistles. I can't understand people who've got land, yet let it lie fallow like that. It would fetch a tidy sum too.'

'True enough, but people aren't so keen on parting with it. Once you let an inheritance go, it's hard to come by another; and it's not everyone who lives till the Jubilee.⁵ If your family and mine had held on to theirs, we might have been a lot better off today.'

'But surely it belongs to somebody, or do you think the owner's dead?'

'He could be, of course, but even so, you'd think he'd have some sons or relatives, who would do something about it.'

'You can never tell,' said the other, 'some of us have got sons and no land, and some have got land and no sons. Just think of Boaz, for instance.'

'Looking at that field, reminds me', said his friend, 'of what Job said, back in the days of Ram,⁶ "If my land has cried out against me, and its furrows have complained with tears . . . if I have eaten its fruits without paying for them, or have caused the rightful owners to breathe their last, let thistles grow instead of wheat and cockleburs instead of barley." '⁷ At that moment a third reaper butted in:

'You want to know who that field belongs to? You can't have been in town very long, else you'd know. That field belongs to Elimelech. It's been like that now, at least ten years. He and his family cleared out down to Moab at the end of the oppression. Never heard of them since. A relative of Boaz, too. Proper nuisance when the thistledown blows but nothing can be done about it. It's his field, and nobody else can touch it.'

'Look out!' somebody shouted, 'here come the donkeys.' The white limestone dust billowed into the air as the beasts of burden went jostling by. They were for carrying the stooks. There was not much for them to do the first day or two, but as the harvest proceeded, the donkeys were busily employed bringing in the sheaves to the threshing floor, which was specially made of beaten soil, at a central point in the open fields.

It always took quite a time to get going the first day, and the sun was well up before the first sickle went in, but once they started, the reapers worked with enthusiasm. After all, it was what they had been waiting for! At some suitable spot a large awning was erected. This was pitched close to one of the wells. Young men were detailed to draw water; and at mealtime, folk would congregate beneath the awning and be issued with rations, or eat perhaps what they had·brought, according as their terms of hire might be.

As the work of the barley harvest got under way, Naomi and Ruth were also toiling, but over hill and dale, on the ascending route to Bethlehem. The journey was most exhausting for Naomi and by the time they reached the approaches of the town she looked so haggard, she might well have collapsed. They came in from the north, by the same road she had taken a decade before. As the sun went down, the fields of barley glowed richly in the fading light. Tired though she was, Naomi felt she had never seen anything quite so beautiful. They went a little farther, and away in the distance, she glimpsed an area of uncultivated land. Its contour was painfully familiar. Yes, it was still there, untouched since the day they left it. A lump rose in her dust-clogged throat as she walked doggedly on, but she said nothing to Ruth. So they went, the two of them together, until they came to Bethlehem. The cycle now was nearing its completion. There had been relapse, reduction and return; now restoration was not far away.

The word 'until' in Scripture bespeaks a God-originated determination. It was up *until* the daybreak that the Angel wrestled with the man called Jacob. The shepherd went on searching *until* he found his wayward sheep. The woman swept her house *until* she grasped her precious piece. God is in earnest. He yearns to find us one by one, and bring us home. This very thing He did for Naomi. The strong intention of His grace had granted resolution to her faith. 'They went', says the text, '*until* they came to Bethlehem.'

The returning reapers mingled with their fellow townsfolk relaxing in the streets. Women stood chatting at their doors or spinning yarn upon their steps. Ruth, the foreigner, and weary Naomi, shuffled slowly through the old north gate. They hardly knew just what to do, or where to stay. But in a moment, every eye was turned towards them. People peered from their houses and others stopped in their tracks. Then an elderly woman came gingerly forward, followed by another, then several more.

'No, it can't be! Not Naomi!' There was a chorus of voices, as with consternation, they looked on the features of their long lost friend, so scarred with suffering. Some were lovingly concerned. Others stood aloof, unable to forget the way she left. It tends to be like that, when anyone comes back to God. Like wildfire, neighbours spread the news, till quite a crowd had gathered round. 'It's Naomi!' some whispered with a hushed surprise. 'But who's that with her?' Some looked askance, resentment glinting in their eyes. It was a trying time for Naomi, and too, for Ruth. They found such scrutiny so hard to bear. They were a spectacle but once the immediate wonder waned, they found a welcome after all. Their move from Moab's fields to Bethlehem had moved the city. Whenever God moves out in grace and souls are moved and drawn to Him, then other souls are moved who see it. The movement back, sets angels singing and makes for 'dancing' in the Father's house. The whole community became affected. '*All* the city was moved,' says the Scripture, and well it might be! When the backslider comes back and the outsider comes in, God runs to meet them. If God so moves, shall puny man be still?

Naomi is profoundly affected. She feels her guilt. There comes again a sense of shame. She dreads their questions. 'Where is Elimelech?' they ask, 'and the boys we knew? Come tell us Naomi, where are they now?'

'O call me not Naomi, she cries, 'but call me Mara. My pleasantness is turned to bitterness. I went out full and the Lord hath brought me home again empty. Why then call ye me Naomi, seeing the Lord hath testified against me, and the Almighty hath afflicted me?'

It was a big price to pay, but in retrospect, it was not too much. The recompense was great. Naomi was home and Ruth was with her. The kindness of the Lord remained. Its taste would prove yet sweeter still.

NOTES

1. This expression 'barley harvest' as used in the Book of Ruth was found also in the Gezer Calendar, which some scholars feel is the most ancient inscription extant in early Hebrew writing. The calendar is reckoned to have been in use perhaps 1000 years before Christ and describes the period of 'barley harvest' as the 'Month of pulling flax. Month of barley harvest. Month when everything (else) is harvested'.
2. 'Shalom' means peace and was a greeting of the period. Cf. Judges 19:20
3. See the references to this in Proverbs 25:13 and 26:1
4. The fact that the servant–steward is described as 'a boy' in the Hebrew, would hardly infer immaturity, but imply rather, subordination to Boaz in the work-relationship. It is simply the masculine form of the word 'damsel' used for Ruth elsewhere in the narrative.
5. Note Leviticus 25:23–28. 'The land shall not be sold for ever ... in the Jubilee it shall go out, and he (the erstwhile owner) shall return unto his possession.'
6. Ram was the great grandson of Judah, and the great grandfather of Salmon the father of Boaz. It is just possible, judging by the character of Elihu, who was of the kindred of Ram, that the Ram of Ruth 4:19 could be the same as the Ram mentioned in Job 32:2. Some, however, would feel that The Book of Job savours too much of patriarchal times for that; and of course, chronologically, the disparity is great.
7. Job 31:38–40

Twelve

Field of Favour

> *'Doubtless thou art our father, though Abraham be ignorant of us, and Israel acknowledge us not: Thou, O Lord, art our father, our Redeemer; Thy name is from everlasting.'*
>
> Isaiah 63: 16
>
> *' When thou cuttest down thine harvest in thy field, and hast forgot a sheaf in the field, thou shalt not go again to fetch it: it shall be for the stranger, for the fatherless, and for the widow: that the Lord thy God may bless thee in all the work of thine hands.'*
>
> Deuteronomy 24: 19

THERE are two books in the Bible that bear the name of women. One is Esther and has to do with the preservation of the people of God. The other is Ruth and has to do with the preservation of the inheritance of God. Both these books have been read down the years at important annual festivals of the Jews. Ruth is read at Pentecost and Esther at Passover. They are peculiarly relevant, for these portions tell us that God not only provides an inheritance for his people but preserves his people to enjoy it. These immortal stories are the songs and sagas of the redeemed.

In The Book of Ruth, her links with Boaz and their development are set out in relation to two particular harvests. She comes into initial favour at the barley harvest; and into ultimate union at the wheat harvest. The barley harvest, which was at Passover time in the Jewish calendar, coincided with the occasion of our Lord's death and resurrection. In fact, on the first day of the week, when our Lord rose again, the first fruits of the barley harvest would be brought to the temple. Christ, the corn of wheat which fell into the ground and died, springs forth in resurrection life to become the firstfruits of them that slept. We, like Ruth, sinners of the Gentiles, first came into favour then.

'God was in Christ reconciling the world unto Himself.' But
the grace of God not only brings us into favour, but has in view
the union of believers with their Kinsman-Redeemer. Thus with
Ruth, we need to look right on to the wheat harvest. This
brings us in the calendar to Pentecost and speaks of the baptism
with the Holy Spirit, which incorporates every redeemed soul
into the body of Christ, making us one with our Lord.[1] It is
one thing to taste the kindness of the Kinsman and to marvel at
His condescension to us as strangers but he would have us
become His very bride and enter consciously into a spiritual
union with Himself, eternal as the love that bought us.

The story we now trace leads us through these fields of
favour, from one harvest to the other. It takes us down by night
to the threshing-floor and then up by day to the gate. It is the
human story in which the very purposes of God are ripening
with the corn. We have trodden the *way out* with Elimelech and
his family; and thought on the *way back* with Naomi; now we
rejoice with Ruth, as she finds a *way in* to the very heart and
fold of God.

There were, needless to say, certain problems confronting
these two women on their arrival at Bethlehem. One was the
question of accommodation. This may have been solved
temporarily, by an offer of hospitality from an old friend,
though Naomi was perhaps too sensitive for that. The story as
related in the Bible, seems to indicate that Naomi and Ruth
found a room of their own. This, of course, could have been
rented, but, on the other hand, may well have been a portion of
the old property that had lain derelict through the intervening
years. They were, at first, far too poor to renovate it, but it
could have provided a refuge during those first few weeks and a
measure of seclusion from overmuch contact with the local
residents, whose enquiries proved so embarrassing. The other
problem, naturally, was that of finding a livelihood. Naomi, in
her tired and distraught condition, was not fit for work, at least
for the present, thus it fell to Ruth to take the initiative, and
seek employment to provide for their needs. The harvest was
obviously bounteous. The only way to taste the good of it was to
get to the fields. Hence, soon after arrival, Ruth says to her
mother-in-law, 'Let me now go to the field, and glean ears of

corn after him in whose sight I shall find grace.' And Naomi
says, 'Go, my daughter!' (2:2). Ruth had emerged from a nation
destined for judgment. Awakened by God and seeking Him
now with all her heart, she believed there was grace awaiting
her in the fields of Bethlehem. Later in the day when she
experienced that grace, her soul was filled with wonder (2:10);
and having once tasted it, her request to Boaz was that she might
continue in it (2:13). This in the words of John is 'grace upon
grace'. The first mention of grace in the Bible is the grace shown
to Noah.[2] It was shown to him as one who lived in the shadow
of wrath. It had been much the same for Ruth. Grace plucks
its objects as brands from the burning. God's grace is always
offered *prior* to judgment. But grace refused, precipitates
judgment; and when it falls, it is always final.

It is refreshing to see for once, the old and the young working
together. That is God's way. Naomi, restored, finds that the
Law sown in her heart as a child, breaks through at last in
wholesome counsel. Ruth, ignorant of much as yet, but fresh
in her first love for Jehovah, is anxious and ready to learn. The
wisdom of old minds, and the love and enthusiasm of young
hearts, make a powerful partnership. Too often today, youth has
zeal without knowledge; and age, a knowledge without vision.
The cleavage is disastrous. Youth and age are indispensable to
each other, but if they would grow up together in Christ, they
need to spend time together, pray together and work together, as
did Moses and Joshua, Elijah and Elisha, and Paul and Timothy.
But if the young will not confess their ignorance, they will never
be wise; and if the old talk always with arrogance, they will
never impart. There is a tendency on the part of the old to
discredit the spiritual exercises of the young. They may be
immature or wrongly interpreted, but not therefore, spurious in
themselves. Eli says to young Samuel, time and again, 'Go and
lie down again'. It was inconceivable to Eli that God should
speak to this novice of a child. What did *he* know? The fact of
the matter is that we do not have to know very much to hear
the voice of God. Even a lamb can hear the shepherd if he
follows closely at his feet. Naomi had voiced the command
'Go!' once before to Ruth. As a backslider, lingering still on the
verge of Jordan, and broken to pieces by her own failure, she

said to her, 'Go, return to your mother's house'. It was an appalling suggestion and a quenching of Ruth's aspirations, although of course, their testing. The old can talk too much like this. 'You go and lie down!' 'You be quiet!' 'You recognise your place and get back to it!' One of the reasons age has such an antipathy to youth is that the questions and enthusiasm of youth, very often, reveal the spiritual bankruptcy of those who are the church's senior citizens. Only in rare circumstances can youth really lead youth. Contrary to the general impression, youth is not really averse to older people as such. True spiritual maturity, superior wisdom and a wider experience is something which youth will respect in their elders. Where an older person by dint of real character, evident gift, and honed ability, shows, under the power of God, what should and can be done, he will find that youth will follow him. Leaders must show self-sacrifice, if they want youth to sacrifice themselves. An effete, indisciplined and self-indulgent set of older people in church prominence, who want to be obeyed simply because they are older, will only earn the disdain of the rising generation. It is useless if we brandish clichés. We need to wield the Spirit's sword. The quixotic is not the apostolic. We err, says our Lord, when we know neither the Scripture or the power of God. Some know the Scriptures but deny the power. Some profess the power but will not bow to Scripture. This is the great divorce that shames His Name. We must take heed to ourselves and the doctrine. Experience must be Bible based and its growth, be Bible tested. We need both the Scriptures and the power of God, but God's power only flows through obedience to His Word. If this is evidenced in older people, young ones will sense reality and follow when so led, but they will never tolerate hypocrisy. As for Naomi, she had now, what Ruth needed and what Ruth gladly acknowledged, namely, a re-collection of the Word of God and an experience of the power of God. Ruth, as the younger person, had what Naomi no longer enjoyed, the vigour for active and prolonged labour that brings in bread. In working together with God, toward the goals of redemption, they both were fed; and in the end, blessed beyond all computation.

Continuing our story we see that Ruth, though a late-comer,

and an in-comer, is nevertheless, covered by the legal provisions
for widows and strangers governing those gleaning in the fields of
Israel. It is precisely here, that Boaz, himself, is introduced. He
is one of their relations, a kinsman we are told, of the family of
Elimelech. We are told, too, of his social station. He is 'a
mighty man of wealth'. For Naomi and Ruth, Boaz stands out as
a person of both affinity and resources, the man to deliver.

Thinking of his affinity, we should note that there are four
different words used for the kinsman relationship which appear
in the second chapter of The Book of Ruth. The word in verse
one is 'moda', and simply means a relative. In verse three, where
Boaz is said to be 'of the kindred of Elimelech', the word is
'mispachah', which means 'one of the family'. In verse twenty,
where we read, 'the man is near of kin', the word is 'qarob',
emphasising his nearness; and the final reference, also in verse
twenty, where Boaz is referred to as 'our next kinsman', the
word is 'gaal', the one with the right to redeem. Ironically in
former days, Elimelech and Naomi tended to view their kinsman Boaz, as a man apart. They had no use for him then and
were far too proud to tell him their problems. Now, however, all
is changed. Boaz only has to step on the stage, and he fills the
scene. There are a host of folk in action but he is the one on
location. In that sense he stands alone in the field. He is to be
the hero of the whole drama, the personality that gives relevance
and substance to all that transpires. Without Boaz nothing
happens. All initiative is in his hands. He is what we might call,
'the personality of increase', the emerging force. The terms
describing him take on strength. The recognition of his stature
and his ways of grace, grow daily greater. This was the apostle's
experience of His heavenly Redeemer. As he looked up into
His face from the Damascus road he saw, as it were, 'a light
from heaven'. When he gives his testimony, he calls it 'a great
light'; and when he gives it again, he speaks of 'a light above the
brightness of the sun'. In writing to the Corinthians he goes even
further and says, it is the God who commanded the light to
shine out of darkness, shining into my heart and yours, in the
face of Jesus Christ. The Person of Christ on the path of the
justified, is as the light of the dawn, that grows and brightens to
the noonday of God. Thus the man Boaz, who at first is only a

relative, is soon called one of the family. He becomes to Naomi
and Ruth, one very near, until finally recognised as their
looked for redeemer. How good it is when our appreciation of
the Lord Jesus Christ is raised to this level. Then we begin to
exclaim, 'There is none other name for me'. Once the person of
Boaz was brought before Naomi and Ruth, the thought of there
being any other kinsman was completely eclipsed. He fills their
horizon. Once John the Baptist saw Jesus and received the
witness of the Spirit as to His identity, he could only say, 'This
is He! Behold the Lamb! He *must* increase . . .' And who
amongst us, of those that love Him, would not endorse that
great imperative?

Boaz, however, is not only a kinsman, he is a mighty man.
He has, as we noted, both affinity and resources. If we think of
his pedigree, his ancestry looks back to Judah through Pharez.
If we think of his posterity, he is linked with Solomon through
David. This genealogy is important to God and He records it,[3]
giving every paternal link between the founder of the tribe and
the establisher of the Kingdom. Solomon was so impressed
with the character, renown and ability of Boaz that he came to
name the brazen pillars that supported the entrance to the
temple, Jachin and Boaz, meaning respectively, 'He shall
establish' and 'In it is strength'.[4] Christ, in His redemptive
right to establish, and his moral strength to uphold, accords to
us, who are aliens to the commonwealth of Israel, an access
through His grace, into the house of God. Boaz, being the
mighty man he was, would through the strength latent in his
kinship, character and resources, uphold for Gentile Ruth, an
entrance into the congregation of Israel. He was sufficient for
her in this, even as Christ is sufficient for us. Jesus alone, can
plead our cause in The Gate, for He suffered without the gate,
paying the price there, that He might have us for ever.

Boaz, then, was mighty in pedigree and mighty in power
(2:1). In him lay a total authority (2:5); and riches of grace
(2:10). He was large in provision (2:14-16); and plenteous in
redemption (4:9). He was mighty in word and in deed; mighty
to save. Yet as in all other types of Christ, Boaz too falls short of
the substance he foreshadows. The comparisons, in the end, only
serve to emphasise the contrast between this noble character

and the noblest One of all. Boaz, in lifting Ruth from poverty
and anonymity, sustained no real impoverishment. Nor yet did
David in his care of Mephibosheth, but when the ultimate
David and the true Boaz, Jesus Christ stepped in to redeem,
we see a mighty man with a difference. He also was a man of
wealth. 'He was rich' says the Scripture, for all things were His
from the beginning, yet to redeem His bride to Himself, he
deliberately became poor, and what poverty was His, that we
through His poverty might become rich.[5]

He is God's Man; yet our Kinsman. He is the One Man who
transforms the scene for the helpless outsider who is yearning
for grace.

> *Thou Who wast rich beyond all splendour,*
> *All for love's sake becamest poor;*
> *Thrones for a manger didst surrender,*
> *Sapphire-paved courts for stable floor.*
> *Thou Who wast rich beyond all splendour,*
> *All for love's sake becamest poor.*
>
> *Thou Who art God beyond all praising*
> *All for love's sake becamest Man;*
> *Stooping so low, but sinners raising*
> *Heavenwards by Thine eternal plan.*
> *Thou Who art God beyond all praising*
> *All for love's sake becamest Man.*[6]

NOTES

1. The first fruits of the barley harvest were offered on the day Jesus rose
   from the dead (Leviticus 23:4–11). The two leavened loaves of the meal
   offering, celebrating the culmination of the wheat harvest, were offered
   on the Day of Pentecost, fifty days following the waving of the barley
   sheaf (Leviticus 23:15–17). And this was the day when the Holy Spirit
   was given and believers from amongst the Jews and Gentile proselytes,
   being incorporated into one Living Body of Christ, became His Church.
   It has been suggested that Naomi and Ruth came into Bethlehem with
   heads bowed like the Barley-ear, but that by the close of harvest their
   heads were erect like ears of wheat.
2. See Genesis 6:8. The word in Genesis for 'grace', is the same as in Ruth
   for 'grace' and 'favour'. It is the Hebrew 'chen'.
3. See Ruth 4:18–22
4. See I Kings 7:21; and II Chronicles 3:17. If we think of Boaz on the
   more personal level, he corresponds in Israel, to those in the church at

Philadelphia, who, though surrounded by Jews of the Synagogue of Satan, nevertheless stood firm under pressure. They 'kept the word of His patience' and did not deny His Name. The overcomer in this context would be made a pillar in the temple of God, and would bear God's Name Rev. 3 : 12. This promise links with Boaz, who stood for God in the famine and filth of his society, which although 'Jewish' had given place to Satan. He was consequently immortalised by his illustrious descendant Solomon, the son of David; 'Boaz' became a brazen pillar in the house of God. It was a fitting acknowledgement for one who had been such a pillar of strength in the house of Israel.

5. II Cor. 8 : 9
6. An excerpt from a poem by Frank Houghton.

Thirteen

The Identification

'*Whose daughter art thou?* Genesis 24:23
'*Whose son art thou?* I Samuel 17:58
'*Who are ye?* Acts 19:15
'*What is thy name?* Genesis 32:27
'*Whose damsel is this?* Ruth 2:5

HAVING been introduced to the man in authority, we are now introduced to his sphere of authority. The figure of Boaz stands now in the field and immediately dominates it. The contrast between Boaz and Ruth at this stage could not be more complete. He has everything. She has nothing. How then does she come to be there? The answer is, by the sovereignty of God; 'her hap', says the text, 'was to light on a part of the field belonging to Boaz'. Happenings are primarily effects, and only subsequently, causes. Events are like islands suddenly appearing in the sea of Time. They are not permanent, but like the eddying currents around them, they come and go. We perceive them, but rarely discern the hidden forces, deep beneath, that make them surface. The will within me, the will of men about me, and the will of Satan to seduce me, all interacting with the will of God to reach me, are the unseen forces that occasion 'our' events. When young Rebekah speaks the words the aged servant prayed she would, he rightly says, 'I being in the way, the Lord led me'. Ruth's choice of field through quiet submission, finds her in the choice of God. It is the one who yields to God, that finds his sovereignty spectacular. His promise stands. 'In all thy ways acknowledge Him and He shall direct thy paths.'

At the first sight of Boaz, we are told 'he came from Bethlehem'. Like the Ancient of Days, whose advent would take up his lineage, he breathes out the truth of the Emmanuel. 'The

Lord be with you,' is his greeting to the reapers. Messiah would fulfil that prayer, and 'God with us' would be His Name. 'The Lord bless thee,' answer the reapers. And in the Christ, all nations of the earth are blessed. These were not Ruth's words, though one day soon, they would be. She was not yet a reaper; only a gleaner. She is not working for Boaz. She works for the good of herself and her mother-in-law. It is one thing to glean in the fields of the Master and gather nourishment for the soul, but it is something greater to be employed by Him as a reaper. It is the progression from an enjoyment of sustenance, to an engagement in service.

Boaz, it is comforting to see, is in touch with his labourers, throughout his field. As their employer, he stands apart, but he is not aloof from them as a man. There is both dignity and sympathy, and it issues in a mutual courtesy that is more than formal, for it savours of endearment. The master-and-servant relationship is never degraded or denounced in Scripture, but sanctified by Him, who, though Master of everything, became a servant. Here He served us well in manhood, and now as man, still serves as Lord. Some men would quickly cease from serving if only they could be a master. Lording and leisure go together; that is their concept. Our task is not to become a master, but to be like our Master, and so serve others even more. Boaz does not leave his reapers to work alone. He is found amongst them in the field where they labour. Throughout history, God has always had a sphere amongst men, where He Himself has visited and been directly operative. Once it was Eden; later it was Israel. In the days of His flesh, it was Christ; and today it is the Church. When the Kingdon of heaven (which at present is a mystery, known only to faith), becomes manifest in millenial glory, then Edenic bloom will be restored to the earth; Israel will be head of the nations; Christ will be King and Priest upon His throne, and the Church at His side will share in His dominion. All the factors of God, operative down the years, will be brought together when at last He reigns over the nations.

Because of who He is, the Lord Jesus Christ must be pre-eminent wherever He is. This is supremely so when we consider the role of the Church, as God's present vehicle of expression in the earth. In the fields of Boaz, no other name is mentioned.

The entire area is his inheritance. His name is excellent in all its borders and in all its corners. It is the same when we look at Christ. He is the appointed heir of all things. His Name is excellent in all the earth. When He stands at Jordan, God's Spirit sees no other man but Jesus, thus on Him rests. When He dies on Calvary, Christ is central to the scene; the other men die nameless, though Jesus dies that they might live. We look to heaven, and Jesus' Name is all the glory. All action in the field begins with Boaz. The field is his. The harvest is his. The reapers are his. The food is his. The rewards are his. So with Christ and His Church. He is the source of all its activity and the wellspring of all its strength. He is the Head of the Body; the Shepherd of the sheep. He is High Priest over the house of God. He is The Lord of the harvest. He gives the seed and gives the increase. He gathers to His barn at last. He is the author and the finisher of faith; the single Lord from whom all service stems. There can be no other name for the Church; no other name in its message; no other name in the field. There is only Jesus. All that is done must be done in that Name.

But how is the intention of Boaz communicated? And how is the harvest gathered to his pleasure? There is a nameless servant, we are told, set over the reapers (2:5). Just as Eliezer went forth as the nameless servant of Abraham, to obtain a bride for Isaac, and in so doing depicted the Holy Spirit proceeding from the Father to win a bride for His Son; so here, this nameless servant, set over the reapers, depicts the Holy Spirit at work in Christ's harvest field. Through Him, the mind of the Master is interpreted and made effectual. Each reaper is appointed to, and entrusted with, a particular task. All direction and correction is given by the nameless servant, in the name of him whose corn it is. It is important to realise that any attempt to reap in the field without the appointment of Boaz's representative, would not only render such reaping invalid, but constitute the unauthorised reaper a common trespasser. All his motives would be suspect. He would be viewed as a thief and a robber who had climbed up some other way. There is no witness or work for God that is independent of the Spirit. *God* has set every member in the Body as it hath pleased Him and given the manifestation of the Spirit to every man to profit withal.[1] Only

that which is born of God can ever be acceptable to God. The
idea of enrolling ourselves in Christ's service and doing what we
like in it, is quite foreign to the New Testament. As His bond-
slaves, we are to do what we are told, and the Holy Spirit is the
One to tell us.

In passing, we also notice that there is no evidence of any
'hierachy' amongst the reapers themselves. Their capacities for
labour must have varied greatly but if faithful in the task
appointed, their reward was sure at the end of the day. Man is an
addict of bureaucracy, and a fanatic for systems. It is such a pity
for God has never viewed them necessary. A leader, it has been
said, is someone who has followers. If a religious leader simply
holds office in some expediently devised ecclesiastical organisa-
tion, his authority will depend on the men who appointed him;
whereas God's way is, that through spiritual stature, a man
should genuinely lead his co-workers and fellow believers
nearer to God; that he should be loved and obeyed as closer to
Christ than they. Each reaper stood in a personal relationship
with Boaz, being engaged quite specifically through the nameless servant on his behalf. They had access to him. He answered
their needs. The rewards were not to officials or teams. God
does not reward people by reason of church office or committee
membership. He rewards every man individually, according to
his work. Nor is it quantity but quality that counts. What
matters is 'of what sort it is'.[2] Motive, faith and continuance,
have much to do with that, not to mention love, without which
all things are worthless. Disciples, saints, servants, followers.
brethren, sisters, witnesses, labourers, builders, priests, shepherds, soldiers, sowers, reapers, waterers. These are the kind of
terms employed to tell of those who believe on the Lord Jesus
Christ and labour with Him in His work. Each apostolic writer,
whatever his authority, chooses in the end to be a bondslave.
The overseers, though called to guide and feed the flock, exist
to serve. They are not lords to feast upon God's heritage. The
offices ordained by God, do not enhance the men who hold
them, much less, the offices by men contrived. The throne does
not itself make monarchs kingly. If power itself be prized, the
present 'gain' is prize enough; for God's rewards rest not in
pride of place, but in the nature of the service rendered. For

'many that are first shall be last', says Jesus, 'and the last shall be first'. God uses whom He will and where. He takes the least esteemed and wields them mightily. And members of the Body, which seem to be more feeble, He proves to be the ones most needful. He takes no stock of human status but looks on him, who, in contrition walks His way. Christ's portion in our hearts, not our position over others, is the crucial thing. Diotrophes loved prominence, Corinthian teachers reigned as kings. But Paul, as less than the least of saints, nor meet, he felt, to be called an apostle, is the man God used. He had no time for any set-up be it Jewish, 'Christian', pagan or political. He gave honour to whom honour was due but all that counted was a new creation. 'If I yet pleased men,' he writes, 'I should not be the servant of Christ.' Only a work born, directed and matured of the Spirit, means anything to Christ. If the reapers of Boaz did stratefy their ranks, or make some foremen of their own, it was all so inconsequential to the harvest, as to be essentially ignored. We shall lead others, only as we are led of Christ. There is absolutely no other reason for fellow-believers to do what we say. We need to beware of the offices of men but ever open to the promptings of the Spirit. As we submit ourselves one to another, the spiritual will emerge to guide. There are gifts to covet[3] and works to desire[4] but no positions to grasp in the Church of God. Our labour is not for getting. All that we reap is for Jesus, and has He not said, 'I will give what is right at the close of the day'. Such teaching is not founded on The Book of Ruth but on the word of our Lord Jesus as expounded by His apostles. The Book of Ruth, however, is like a little window, through which the light of God pours in, to clarify truth seen elsewhere.

If we keep the window open, we shall find that the analogy develops as Boaz speaks his opening words to Ruth. We see now that it is the nameless servant who introduces Boaz to Ruth, and Ruth to Boaz. A blest reminder that it was the Holy Spirit who first introduced our Redeemer to us and introduced us to our Redeemer. Without that introduction none of us could have recognised Him or come to know Him. In this connection it is important to note also that it was Boaz who first enquired of Ruth. It was he who approached her. Ruth only

enquired after him, and approached him, in consequence of his
advance to her. Christ seeks us when we are strangers before
we ever seek for Him. He chooses us; it is not so much that we
choose Him. 'We love Him,' says John, 'because He first loved
us.' How unstrained and consistent are the illustrations of
Scripture.

The first matter to be raised by Boaz in his contact with Ruth,
is the question of her identity. 'Whose damsel is this?' In a
feudal society everyone is linked with a family. There is no
one really unattached. Spiritually speaking, in present day
society, this is equally true. Either God or the devil is our
father. Our Lord Jesus was quite unequivocal about that.[5]
It is the kind of question Eliezer asked Rebekah, 'Whose
daughter art thou?' And the kind of question Saul asked David,
'Whose son art thou?' Such probing of identity brings us to
definition. It is always the Spirit who defines us to God and who
defines us to ourselves. The servant defines Ruth categorically.
He says, 'It is the Moabitish damsel'. That is what she was
after the flesh. 'Who came back with Naomi out of the country
of Moab.' That is what she was by faith. There is a realm into
which we are born and there is a Kingdom into which we are
born again. The far country spoke of what she was by nature;
the fields of Boaz, of the hopes now proffered her in grace. This
is the servant's initial testimony to Ruth. She was obtaining a
witness and that is the first step to becoming a witness. If the
Spirit can testify of our works, then our faith is real. This is
what the servant now proceeds to do. He reports what she had
said to him and what she had done, that is her words and her
deeds. First of all, she took nothing for granted. She made
request to the right quarter and did not presume. Secondly she
acknowledged her place. She did not claim to be a reaper but
just a poor gleaner, one who was a stranger within the gates,
seeking a bounty to which she had no right, save under the
mercy latent in the Law.

Having obtained permission to glean, she commended herself
to the servant of Boaz by her diligence and continuance. She had
a right proportion of things. Apart from a brief pause for rest
'in the house',[6] that is, under the awning, she had laboured all
morning. For some it was mostly rest and little work. For Ruth

it was mostly work and little rest. She knew why she was there, and the rest she took was only to enable her to work more effectively. The believer can only rest in Time as a means to an end. Rest is never an end in itself on earth. But when all is finished and God is satisfied with His new heavens and new earth, then we shall rest with Him, and out of that rest, serve Him for ever. The rest in heaven is a rest from earthly labours for all who were formally heavy laden and who came to Jesus. From our eternal state of equilibrium, however, we shall enter upon divine projects of unimagined scale, and will do so with unfailing energy. Like the angels, fed of God, we shall never tire. Did not the Israelites have a foretaste of this when they ate angel's food in the wilderness. Such thoughts should stimulate us as we labour in the Master's fields and tread the pilgrim way. 'There remaineth a rest for the people of God.' That rest is in Christ who has already sat down. He would not have us weary for ever.

> *Rise, my soul! thy God directs thee;*
> *Stranger hands no more impede;*
> *Pass thou on; His hand protects thee,*
> *Strength that has the captive freed.*
>
> *Though thy way be long and dreary,*
> *Eagle strength He'll still renew;*
> *Garments fresh and foot unweary*
> *Tell how God hath brought thee through.*
>
> *There no stranger God shall meet thee;*
> *Stranger thou in courts above!*
> *He who to His rest shall greet thee,*
> *Greets thee with a well-known love.*[7]

With her identity now defined, Boaz speaks directly to the one he seeks. He immediately challenges her conscience. He infers that she would just as soon glean otherwhere. 'Hearest thou not my daughter?' he says. Or as one version puts it. 'Listen my daughter, Go not to glean in another field, neither go from hence, but abide here fast by my maidens.' Ruth does not resent the seeming abruptness of this approach, but only

marvels at his interest. He seems to know her through and
through, for truly she was in his field, not for his sake but for
her own. She would in fact go anywhere, if only Naomi and
she could be sustained. As yet she had no sense of loyalty
towards Boaz. She did not know him, though he took knowledge of her low estate. Christ knew what was in man, neither
would he commit Himself to man. He knew who would betray
him and who would believe on Him. What encouragement He
gave to those the Father drew. They would be His gift. Yet
many today have the spiritual wanderlust and no conscience
about it. They flit from field to field, if not from faith to faith.
They are like butterflies, sipping of nectar here and tasting it
there. The nomadic spirit grips the saints. As pilgrims they
should go from strength to strength but as nomads they go from
church to church looking for the greenest pasture. As for the
harvest field, some never graduate from gleaners to reapers but
snatching a few grains from one communion, haste on to the
next. There is no real attachment formed to the Redeemer, or
the seeking of His mind as to how and where, or with whom to
gather for worship and labour. The reason is not hard to find. It
is because they enter a church fellowship to gain rather than to
give. The church connection is viewed more as an opportunity
for mental re-charging and social contact, than a scene of
exercise and responsibility in the adoration and service of God.
If we light upon a field where the grain is the fruit of God's
seed and the ears are full; where the Redeemer is the joy of all
the labourers and His good pleasure their business; then having found it, it is well to remain there. That, in effect, is what
Boaz says to Ruth. 'Don't you go anywhere else, now you are in
my field. You stay with my maidens.' This is the fellowship
of virgin hearts. These maidens represented a vigorous company, which Boaz could trust. They knew how to work and to
reap, and their friendship would prove most helpful to Ruth. If
her eyes were focussed where their eyes were focussed, she
would not go far wrong. 'Let thine eyes be on the field that they
do reap and go thou after them.' That was his wisdom. Paul
could say, 'Be lovers of good men;' and 'Be ye followers of me
as I also am of Chrirt.' To the Thessolonians he wrote, 'ye
became followers of us, and of the Lord, having received the

word in much affliction, with joy of the Holy Ghost: so that ye were ensamples to all that believe ... (and) followers of the churches of God.' Those who turned from the Gentiles in those days, followed after the reapers and kept their eyes on the field that the apostles reaped. The result was that they took on the perspectives, concepts and values of those who had a virgin-affection for Christ. The result was, that such converts did not merely feed on the portions dropped by the workers, but were eventually incorporated in the reaper-band and went on to be labourers together with God.

Boaz now gives Ruth a reassurance. She needs this, for she is in the kind of position where the young men might take advantage of her. She is a foreigner. She is a young widow without a livelihood. There is no one to avenge her, if wronged. She could be an easy prey when the shadows fell and she walked away under the harvest moon. Boaz is aware of every danger. He had sought to forestall any inordinate advance. The young men of whom he speaks had their virtues but they also had their weakness. Any one of them could let his flesh rise up, and humble Ruth. This would be infamous in the fields of Boaz. It was something he could not tolerate. Yet how obliging and helpful these young men could be. They were the men who drew the water for the labourers to drink. They would do it willingly for Ruth, a girl they otherwise would harm, if passion once prevailed. None are so strong they cannot fall. Sometimes the very ones who draw so deeply from salvation's wells, and truly minister it to others, are those whose passion drags them down. What utter chaos and disgrace such sin incurs. What ruin in the ranks of those who gather in the sheaves for Christ! Because there is the flesh and the Spirit in every believer, our Lord, like Boaz, warns against the dangers of indulgence and license. The spiritually active, because of their many contacts are more morally vulnerable than generally believed. 'I have charged the young men', says Boaz, 'that they shall not touch thee.' The word also means 'to plague'. 'It is good', says the apostle, 'for a man not to touch a woman.' It is in the touch, so often, that a man is taken, and a woman marred. Marriage is honourable, being divinely ordained, 'and the bed undefiled'. By all means let every man have his own wife and every wife her own

husband, but outwith that, there is a 'touching' which is to be
abhorred. The world today is full of inordinate and unwarranted
intimacies between people who have no intention of marriage.
Is it not better that we fill our vessels from the springs of God,
than philander in harvest under pretext of service?

The damsel, Ruth, is deeply aware of Boaz in his provision
and protection. She is utterly overwhelmed that such a man
should take cognizance of her. 'She falls on her face' before him.
This is her spontaneous reaction. But then it says, 'she bowed
herself to the ground'. And that was a deliberate action. Both
are precious to Boaz, even as our conscious and unconscious
responses to Christ gladden His heart. 'Why have I found grace
in thine eyes,' she asks, 'seeing I am a stranger?' This sort of
question is not an investigation into the psychology of a land-
owner. It is the 'why' out of which the worship of love is born.
As Christians we are bound to consider the doctrines of grace,
but if we bring to our questing, the sophisticated audacity of the
laboratory and seminar, we shall get nowhere. The analysis of
the mind is nothing, if the heart is not moved. An intellectual
'why' is just an impious insult to the Most High God and puts
'Z' to our spiritual apprehension. We can only say 'Why?' to
the Almighty, if we are on our faces and bowed to the earth.
More things are learned in worship than in the 'workshop'.
There are realities the heart perceives that come via other routes
than reason. In reality, nothing is learned from God without
the attitude of worship. His grace and glory must consume us,
ere we start to think as He does. He does not even look at men
until they tremble at His Word.[8]

> *I cannot tell why He, whom angels worship,*
> *Should set His love upon the sons of men,*
> *Or why as shepherds, He should seek the wanderers,*
> *To bring them back, they know not how or when . . .*
>
> *But this I know, He heals the broken-hearted,*
> *And stays our sin, and calms our lurking fear,*
> *And lifts the burden from the heavy laden.*
> *For yet the Saviour, Saviour of the world, is here.*[9]

NOTES

1. I Corinthians 12 : 18 and 7
2. I Corinthians 3 : 13
3. I Corinthians 12 : 31 ; 14 : 39
4. I Timothy 3 : 1
5. John 8 : 41–44
6. The word in Ruth 2 : 7, although generally translated 'house' is used loosely for woven 'hangings' in II Kings 23 : 7; and 'the spider's web' in Job 8 : 14.
7. An excerpt from a hymn written by J. N. Darby.
8. Isaiah 66 : 1–2
9. An excerpt from the poem by William Y. Fullerton.

Fourteen

Under His Wings

> *'In the shadow of Thy wings will I make my refuge,
> until these calamities be overpast. I will cry unto God
> most high; unto God that performeth all things for me.'*
>
> Psalm 57: 1, 2

WHEN Ruth's head is found at his feet, Boaz discloses his foreknowledge of her case. 'It hath fully been shewed me', he says,
'all that thou hast done unto thy mother-in-law since the death
of thine husband: and how thou hast left thy father and thy
mother, and the land of thy nativity, and art come unto a people
which thou knewest not heretofore. The Lord recompense thy
work, and a full reward be given thee of the Lord God of Israel,
under whose wings thou art come to trust.'[1]

As an answer to Ruth's question, 'Why have I found grace in
thine eyes . . .?' it might at first appear that she had merited this
favour. But if grace is merited, it is no more grace. It will be
remembered that when the angel spoke to Cornelius, who, like
Ruth, was a Gentile and thus an alien to Israel, he said, 'Thy
prayers and thine alms are come up for a memorial before God.'[2]
In view of this disposition of heart towards God, he was given
the opportunity of hearing the Gospel. The emphasis in his
spiritual exercises, is, however, not on 'merit' but on 'memorial'.
God's attention, as it were, is drawn to those that seek Him, and
we know it is those who diligently seek Him whom He thus
rewards. He is 'reminded' of His promise to bless all nations
through Jesus Christ, the Seed of Abraham and the glory of
Israel. The prayers and alms of Cornelius were really the
evidence of his aspiration. They were not the ground of his
salvation, otherwise Peter's preaching of the Gospel would have
been unnecessary. In the case of Ruth, her renunciation of her
background, devotion to Naomi and preference for Jehovah, all

declared that she was ripe for a grace that would bring her into the congregation of Israel. As a Moabitess, this was something barely possible under Law; but what the Law could not do, grace would do. Boaz, who had seen this grace effective in his mother Rahab, granted her a place in his field. One day he would clasp her to his bosom, for had she not already a place in his heart? Her deeds were as a memorial, expressing her willingness and desire before God. His grace shown to her through Boaz would take her up as she was when the moment came, and make her all He wanted her to be. As the Scripture says, 'In every nation, he who has a reverential fear for God is sure of being received and welcomed (by Him).'[3] 'For he is not a Jew, which is one outwardly, ... but he is a Jew, which is one inwardly; and circumcision is that of the heart, in the spirit, and not in the letter; whose praise is not of men, but of God.'[4] The time would come when Ruth would not be found standing in her own name, for no Moabite could stand as such before the Lord. She would stand in the name of Boaz. She would be accepted in her beloved. Any links after the flesh she might claim with Israel through Elimelech and his son Mahlon would be as dead as the men themselves. But by his act of redemption, Boaz would make that which was dead live again in Israel and by that same act, she would live also and take her place in the congregation, as one of God's own. She had shown, by her actions, the aspirations of her heart. It brought her like Cornelius into remembrance, but it was only grace that could give her a standing. What Boaz says here, therefore, prepares our minds for what he later on, so effectually performs.

At this stage the emphasis is chiefly on foreknowledge. This is the first link in the chain of grace. It is always startling to the one addressed, to realise that He who bestows favour knows the end from the beginning. It was to be expected that Boaz should be aware of the background and character of the harvest girls he employed, but Ruth is acutely conscious that in every way she is different from them. 'I am not like one of thine handmaidens,' is something she immediately confesses. Yet Boaz knew all about her just the same. It was this that startled Nathanael. 'Whence knowest Thou me?' he says to Jesus. 'Before that Philip called thee, when thou wast under the fig

tree, I saw thee,' came the answer. And as for the Samaritan
woman at the well, she is so amazed at Christ's understanding of
her past, that she runs away into the town crying, 'Come, see a
man, which told me all things that ever I did: is not this the
Christ?' If we look again at Romans, we find, that those who are
glorified for ever are those who are justified on earth; and that
those who are justified on earth, are those who were called in
Time, after the pre-ordaining of God; but as we go back further
still, we find that this ordering of things by which they heard
His call, was all rooted in foreknowledge. Our Lord could say of
us even before the world began, 'it hath fully been shown me all
that thou hast done.' When He meets us in Time, we feel
surprised to be caught up in something that has its origins prior
to our existence. We begin to see in a new way, how 'all things
work together for good to them that love God, to them who
are the called according to His purpose.'[5] It was this kind of
thing that Ruth was now beginning to discover. She could not
understand how it could be; but somehow Boaz knew. This
mysterious person who had first pierced her conscience now
spoke to her heart. That is the force of the words, 'thou hast
spoken friendly to thine handmaiden'. Boaz interprets to her,
the faith begotten within her. He invokes the divine blessing.
He tells her of 'the Lord God of Israel', the One of whom
she had dreamed in youth, and for whom she had longed as
far back as she could remember. 'Under His wings', says
Boaz, 'you have come to trust, that is, you have taken refuge.'
It is all so reassuring. She begins to know in Whom she has
believed.

In saying some of the things he did, Boaz was speaking from
experience. As a true Israelite, he had sought the guidance of
the Lord in trouble and had been satisfied in drought. He had
not absconded in the crisis of famine, nor turned opportunist
when the oppression broke. He had vowed in his heart what
the Psalmist later penned, 'In the shadow of Thy wings will I
make my refuge, until these calamities be overpast.'[6] There he
had been abundantly satisfied with the fatness of God's house
and had drunk, when all was dry, of the rivers of His pleasure.[7]
The shadow of His wings had been his help and the place of
rejoicing.[8] Covered there with His feathers, he had trusted in

the loving-kindness of the Lord.⁹ Beneath such wings Ruth had now come to trust. How often in days gone by Jehovah would have gathered Elimelech and his family, but they would not. The result? Their house was left to them desolate. Yet Ruth, a child of accursèd Moab, finds her rest, where those who bore the name of an Israelite had spurned to dwell. His wings would be her secret place; she would dwell for ever under the shadow of the Almighty.

All the birds in the Bible that symbolise God are designedly female. The Dove broods as a mother-bird over the chaos of the primordial deep. There the Spirit works to 'vivify and fructify' until an ordered world appears. The eagle-mother bearing her young upon her wings, tells of Jehovah's care for Israel. The hen and her brood is the simile our Lord adopts to bring to mind His ceaseless pleadings with His people. The concepts of the male and female originate, of course, with God. As a father, He pities us, His children.¹⁰ 'As one whom his mother comforteth', He vows, 'so will I comfort you.'¹¹ When father and mother forsake, we are told, the Lord will take us up.

As sheltering beneath His wings and having this truth ministered to her by Boaz, it is little wonder that Ruth exclaims, 'Let me find favour in Thy sight, my lord; for thou hast comforted me and spoken to my heart.'

NOTES

1. Ruth's step is reminiscent, in character and consequence, of Abram's departure from Ur at the call of God. It was a step of faith. Because she believed God, she also is a 'child of Abraham', the father of all who believe. Romans 4:11.
2. See Acts 10:4 and 31
3. See Acts 10:35 in *The Amplified New Testament*.
4. See Romans 2:28, 29
5. Our Lord's comments in Matthew 11:21–22 show how He knew what the reactions of people would be had they had the opportunities, which in fact they were denied. God's choices are always made with all the facts in view. It is only men with their limitations who indulge in prejudice and inflict injustice. There is, however, no reason to presume that foreknowledge is the only factor in determining the divine choice.
6. Psalm 57:1
7. Psalm 36:7
8. Psalm 63:7

9. Psalm 91 : 4
   All these Scriptures refer to the wings of God and speak respectively of
   that secret place as a place of refuge; a place of refreshment; a place of
   rejoicing; and a place of repose.
10. Psalm 103 : 13
11. Isaiah 66 : 13

Fifteen

Handfuls of Purpose

> '*I sat down under his shadow with great delight, and his fruit was sweet to my taste. He brought me to the banqueting house, and his banner over me was love.*'
>
> Canticles 2: 3, 4
>
> '*O taste and see that the Lord is good.*'
>
> Psalm 34: 8

HAVING spoken to her conscience and to her heart, Boaz now satisfies her hunger. 'At mealtime, come thou hither,' he says, 'and eat of the bread, and dip thy morsel in the vinegar.' Like a fledgling from an alien nest, Ruth had been welcomed, stranger though she was, into the warmth and comfort of Israel's mother-hearted God. Enjoying the shelter and protection of the home-born chicks, she is invited to share their food. This is the children's bread and the master's table. She had hoped for a crumb through the toil of her gleaning, but here she was, sitting amongst the reapers and feasting with them; and all this at the request of Boaz. In the Christian life, we start with faith in Christ, but go on to feed from the hand of Christ. As to faith, we believe individually, but when we feed, we are encouraged to feast with others around our mutual Lord. Ruth here is a gleaner amongst the reapers; a Moabitess amongst Israelites, and a woman in widow's garments favoured by brideless Boaz. It speaks of a grace that proceeds; a grace that saves to the uttermost, a grace that perfects its purpose, and maintains for ever, those it chooses to secure.

We see then, that after trusting, there comes the table. This table is different from any other. It is the table of Boaz, the one she has called, 'my lord'. When we use the word table we do not refer so much to a piece of furniture, for under the awning in the field, folk may simply have gathered round and partaken of a buffet meal. We have in mind rather, a company of people who stood in a special relationship to Boaz, the lord of the harvest, and who found fellowship together in his presence as they partook of his provision. Not that the people were the table, of course. The table was rather that constant availability of sustenance proceeding from himself to them, who were his people. Although in the life of the Church, on particular occasions and in particular locations, a tangible table is spread and we refer to what is placed upon it as the Lord's Supper, it is in actual fact, an expression of that broader concept in the Bible, the Lord's Table. Whereas the Lord's supper has a physical content and is limited to time and place, the Lord's table is not dependent on the presence of the material emblems but implies an abiding fellowship with the Lord in all that He is and all that He provides. When we eat of the Lord's supper we show forth the Lord's death. The gathering disperses and we go our ways. But the Lord's Table is in continuous session. It infers a constant feasting upon Him and a living by His life. To be found eating of the Lord's Table does not depend on the convening of a meeting. We can partake of its meat in the presence of our enemies. We do not have to congregate in some suitable building. The Lord can furnish His table in the wilderness. The Lord's supper is only till He come, but we shall still be eating from our Lord's Table in His Kingdom yet to be. That this is a Scriptural distinction is made clear in I Corinthians, where the Lord's Table is set in contrast to the table of demons, a table which is also continually spread and is not necessarily tangible. To whom then do we look, and on whose meat do we feed? 'Ye cannot drink the cup of the Lord, and the cup of devils,' writes Paul. 'Ye cannot be partakers of the Lord's Table and of the table of devils.' Ruth could look back and remember the image of Chemosh, with its outstretched arms of brass in which the sacrifice was burnt. The votive cup of that idolatry was her father's fellowship. The godshelf and its food, was the table from which he chose to eat. She had renounced it all. She had meat to eat that Moab knew not of.[1] Her communion was with Jehovah and His people. The mealtime of Boaz was a sweet expression of all this. She was tasting the master's bread in the fellowship of his reapers. It is possible to have partaken of the Lord's Table and never to have partaken of the Lord's supper, as did the dying thief. But we can never really partake of the Lord's supper until we have eaten of His Table, for if we have never had fellowship with Him in the bonds of life, we can never show forth His death in the fellowship of His people. It is interesting to note, therefore, even in the limitations of this story, that Ruth only fed at the table, when her faith had been attested.[2]

It is not suggested for one moment that the Old Testament scene provides a charter for New Testament Church conduct; but here is a cameo which catches the heart and lights up the believers' privilege. It was Christ, Himself, who laid down the teaching of the Table and the Supper. Then Luke and Paul expounded it in The Acts and the Epistles. The tables of Joseph, Boaz, David and Solomon, however, move us today with wonder and gratitude as we think of how the sons of Jacob, Ruth of Moab, Mephibosheth and the Queen of Sheba were all so bountifully fed. Each in their own way had no claim upon the resources and fellowship of their benefactors, yet through grace, they received a portion and a place.

The fare upon the table of Boaz is suggestive, to say the least, for there is both bread and vinegar. The first mention of bread in The Book of Ruth had to do with the Lord's visitation to Bethlehem. The bread on the table of Boaz would, on reflection, remind Ruth of the good news that first touched their hearts away in Moab. The Lord's supper too, is first concerned with bread. It tells of Him who visited us, the Bread of God come down from heaven; of the One who was ever God, yet became flesh, that He might give His flesh for the life of the world. We think of Him who took up a body at Bethlehem, and offered it up on the Hill. The Supper is that blessed ordinance in which the varied aspects of His gracious visitation are all preserved. In all His ways and all His days we trace His pathway to the tree. But, this is not the morbid commemoration of a dead Inaugurator. It is the worship of a Living Liberator. It is the *Lord's* death we proclaim. The one who died has risen again and gone above, that He might be Lord both of the living and the dead. We do it till He comes. He visited us, but we partake in confidence, for He will visit us again. On the ground of His perfect

work done for us, He will then perfect His work begun in us.
We eat as waiting for the redemption of the purchased possession when our body will be like His, save for the scars. Ruth only
ate in the field, until redemption in all its aspects had been
completed. Then Boaz having done the kinsman's part received
her to his house for ever. So we eat, looking for that day, when
we shall no longer spread the Supper on the floor of the open
field, but eat anew with Him, at His kingdom table. Then we
shall dwell in the house of the Lord for ever and go out no more.

After the bread, the vinegar is mentioned. It is the Hebrew,
'chomets', and indicates a drink made from sour, or unripe
grapes. So in the New Testament the cup of wine follows on the
eating of the bread. First the body given, then the blood out-
poured. A life lived out and a life laid down. Born to be broken,
and broken to bleed. A perfect life in the body achieving a
perfect atonement in death.

The Lord's supper is a divine memorial set up, character-
istically, prior to the enactment of the event, a fact which
distinguishes it from the memorials of men, who boast of
prowess, only after the deed is done. As in the Passover, so in
the Lord's supper; He said what He was going to do, set up the
memorial and then went forth to do it. But whether we think
of Baptism or the Lord's Supper, these two ordinances can
never impart eternal life. The Life that God imparts is never in
the symbol. This Life is in His Son. The ordinances that Christ
established, both speak of death. In Baptism we proclaim the
death of the believer with Christ, and in the Lord's supper, the
death of Christ for the believer. But although the ordinances do
not impart life, they both lead on to life. Baptism, to a newness of
life against which sin has no power; and the Lord's supper, to
that life against which wrath asserts no claim. Practically and
judicially, the ordinances declare God's fullest provision for His
own in time and Eternity, in the Person and Work of His Son.
It is this that makes the ordinances a means of grace. There is
pleasure for Him as faith worships and remembers. There is
everything for us, for Christ is our portion. The Gospel is
preached and angels instructed; and the devil is told once again
of his doom.

It was surely Ruth's genuine appreciation of his kindness that meant so much to Boaz. This made the feast for him. It gladdened his heart. Ruth did not take her privilege for granted but ate with wonder. He wondered too. She might have come with a proletariat bitterness, to grasp and grab. She might have thus inferred that Israel and her princes owed her a living. She might have grudged her social loss and said but I'm as good as you are. But this is absent. All that she does is rest in his grace and joy in his goodness. He wants her to get the very best. To those that value it God gives it. 'Eat of the bread,' says Boaz, 'and dip thy morsel in the vinegar.' This was something at the meal she was to do personally and intelligently. It was a conscious relating of the bread to the vinegar. In our celebration of the Lord's supper we sometimes so separate the bread from the wine in our thinking, that the blood of Christ which has its value by reason of the life lived in the Body, tends to be under-estimated. The Bible speaks of the 'precious blood of Christ'. This is Peter's term and he uses the word also of 'precious promises' and 'precious faith'. Let the thought of all that Jesus did in His body prepared, preserved and presented, evaluate for us the preciousness of the blood that flowed, when that body was given. Let the one, as it were, come in contact with the other. But this requires something from us personally. Boaz could have dipped the bread for Ruth, but he did not do it. He said, 'you do it'. So it is 'the bread which *we* break'. We do it together, but we also do it individually. It is the cup which *we* bless'. Though acting together, each one of us is drinking of the cup in turn. Both corporately and personally we are show-ing forth His death until He come. Unless we bring discern-ment to the supper, this mealtime with our Lord will be reduced to a mere attending of communion and a dispensing of the elements. And what is more serious, we are in danger of eating and drinking to our condemnation.

Once Boaz saw that Ruth was rejoicing in what was set before her, he did something rather more special. He reached her parched corn. Barley was the common fare of the peasantry and Ruth along with the reapers was thankful for it. Thomson in his standard work, *The Land and the Book*, says that the Midianites called the oppressed and impoverished Israelites in Gideon's day, mere 'barley eaters'. It was a derisive term. It gives meaning however to the fact that God used the 'barley cake' of Gideon's few to vanquish their host. The simple fare of the Lord's supper may be despised by the world as poor and meagre but the truth of which the emblems speak, will bring the universe to its knees. As she eats the simple fare, Ruth suddenly receives this richer portion. Something that is fresh, yet has passed through the fire. It was probably grain of the newly cut ears, briefly roasted, although it has been suggested that this was maize, the food of the rich. In showing Ruth this favour, Boaz was dealing with her altogether beyond her station. He was viewing her not so much as she was, but as, one day, God would make her to be. At the Lord's supper we may have many thoughts in common with others, wholesome thoughts, which form the staple diet of God's people; but then there are also treasured moments of realisation, when our Lord, by His own hand, brings to our hearts meat that is especially rich. Then it is we see things concerning Himself and His work that we have never seen before, and in the strength of that meat we take our pilgrimage for many days. Most of us, however, cannot take too much of this at any one time. Once she had partaken of so rich a portion, Ruth was quickly satisfied. It is good to see how she bestirs herself and with renewed energy gets on with her work. She does not sit about, frittering away precious hours under the awning, expatiating on how delightful it was to eat with Boaz. The good food activates her for labour. Meditation that strengthens and sends forth again to service is healthy; but a pietism that makes us withdrawn and inactive is eventually suspect; and especially so if it makes us 'superior'. Ruth is exemplary in this regard. She rested and fed awhile. That was enough. Now she works till the sun goes down. It is wonderful what we can do, when our soul is satisfied with Jesus.

She has been growing in grace and in the knowledge of her kinsman, though as yet, she barely knows him. Having spent time now at his table, she finds his help more present in the field. She began the day picking up grains; she ends the day picking up sheaves. God is a rewarder of diligence, and is certainly so in the field of the Redeemer. The one who has found grace is shown more grace. To the one who 'has', more is given. As the soul proves itself in the few things, it is entrusted with greater things. It is needful at first to receive but little, lest we abuse our privilege, but once the little is taken up wisely, we are entrusted with more. The same diligent spirit that took Ruth through the day, is now in evidence at the end of the day. Some like the man in the Proverbs, are too lazy to roast what they take in hunting, but there is nothing like that about Ruth. What she has gleaned she values. Although weary, she takes time to beat out the ears she has gathered, until an ephah of barley is her reward.[3]

How much more we would profit, if we would only evaluate the data we collate, the light we receive, the ministry we hear, the truth we read and the things we experience. Yet the fatigue incurred in labour, is often our excuse for neglecting its fruit. Gleaning is something that makes us bow down, but threshing makes us perspire. Many do not like that, but the fact remains, that only what is beaten can be eaten,[4] and only what is winnowed can be shared. Billy Bray in the Cornish vernacular and Spurgeon in more polished speech, both remarked, 'Some believers have less sense than a chicken. A hen will pick over a whole bushel of chaff to find one grain of wheat; while others will pick over a whole bushel of wheat to find a little bit of chaff!' Ruth, however, shows us the way. What she gleaned she beat; and what she beat she measured; and what she measured, she took home to her mother-in-law. As far as we can tell, not a grain was left behind. It was the beginning of a course, which, in the end, would find her possessor of the whole field under Boaz. Value first a grain of truth and one day all the inheritance can be yours.

'What has chaff in common with the wheat?' says the Lord.[5] That is an ancient question which we ought to answer; although we rarely do.

NOTES

1. In view of this it is all the more appalling to read that Solomon, Ruth's renowned descendant, in the days of his departure from God, built an high place for Chemosh, the abomination of Moab, in the hill that is before Jerusalem. See I Kings 11 : 6–8.
2. Luke 22 and I Corinthians 10 deal more with the Lord's table. I Corinthians 11 refers to the Lord's supper. Literature on 'The Lord's Supper' by A. P. Gibbs is especially recommended.

3. An ephah is about four gallons. It was ten times more than the quantity of manna the children of Israel gathered in a day. The manna speaks of Christ on earth (See John 6). The old corn of the land speaks of Christ in heaven, our inheritance and portion there. It is good to think on Christ in His pathway here; but if we are to be properly nourished we must feed upon Him where He is, at God's right hand (Colossians 2 : 19).

4. It has been well pointed out that nearly all those things which speak of the appreciation of Christ in the Old Testament, at some time or another are beaten, for example, the manna, the olive, the ingredients of the holy ointment, the incense, and the gold of the candlestick. It tells us that the knowledge of Christ is always bought at a price; though Christ Himself is the gift of gifts.

5. Jeremiah 23 : 28

A NIGHT ON THE THRESHING FLOOR

And she took it up, and went into the city: and her mother in law saw what she had gleaned: and she brought forth, and gave to her that she had reserved after she was sufficed.

And her mother in law said unto her, Where hast thou gleaned today? and where wroughtest thou? blessed be he that did take knowledge of thee. And she shewed her mother in law with whom she had wrought, and said, The man's name with whom I wrought to day is Boaz.

And Naomi said unto her daughter in law, Blessed be he of the Lord, who hath not left off his kindness to the living and to the dead. And Naomi said unto her. The man in near of kin unto us, one of our next kinsmen.

And Ruth the Moabitess said, He said unto me also, Thou shalt keep fast by my young men, until they have ended all my harvest.

And Naomi said unto Ruth her daughter in law, It is good, my daughter, that thou go out with his maidens, that they meet thee not in any other field.

So she kept fast by the maidens of Boaz to glean unto the end of barley harvest and of wheat harvest; and dwelt with her mother in law.

Then Naomi her mother in law said unto her, My daughter, shall I not seek rest for thee, that it may be well with thee?

And now is not Boaz of our kindred, with whose maidens thou wast? Behold, be winnoweth barley to night in the threshingfloor.

Wash thyself therefore, and anoint thee, and put thy raiment upon thee, and get thee down to the floor: but make not thyself known unto the man, until he shall have done eating and drinking.

And it shall be, when he lieth down, that thou shalt mark the place where he shall lie, and thou shalt go in, and uncover his feet, and lay thee down; and he will tell thee what thou shalt do.

And she said unto her, All that thou sayest unto me I will do.

And she went down unto the floor, and did according to all that her mother in law bade her.

And when Boaz had eaten and drunk, and his heart was merry, he went to lie down at the end of the heap of corn: and she came softly, and uncovered his feet, and laid her down.

And it came to pass at midnight, that the man was afraid, and turned himself: and, behold, a woman lay at his feet.

And he said, Who art thou? And she answered, I am Ruth thine handmaid: spread therefore thy skirt over thine handmaid; for thou art a near kinsman.

And he said, Blessed be thou of the Lord, my daughter: for thou hast shewed more kindness in the latter end than at the beginning, inasmuch as thou followedst not young men, whether poor or rich.

And now, my daughter, fear not; I will do to thee all that thou requirest: for all the city of my people doth know that thou art a virtuous woman.

And now it is true that I am thy near kinsman: howbeit there is a kinsman nearer than I.

Tarry this night, and it shall be in the morning, that if he will perform unto thee the part of a kinsman, well; let him do the kinsman's part: but if he will not do the part of a kinsman to thee, then will I do the part of a kinsman to thee, as the Lord liveth: lie down until the morning.

And she lay at his feet until the morning: and she rose up before one could know another. And he said, Let it not be known that a woman came into the floor.

Also he said, Bring the vail that thou hast upon thee, and hold it. And when she held it, he measured six measures of barley, and laid it on her: and she went into the city.

And when she came to her mother in law, she said, Who art thou, my daughter? And she told her all that the man had done to her.

And she said, These six measures of barley gave he me; for he said to me, Go not empty unto thy mother in law.

Then said she, Sit still, my daughter, until thou know how the matter will fall: for the man will not be in rest, until he have finished the thing this day.

Sixteen

Relationship Extraordinary

'*A gracious woman retaineth honour.*'

Proverbs 11 : 16

'*Who can find a virtuous woman? for her price is far above rubies.*'
'*A woman that feareth the Lord, she shall be praised.*'

Proverbs 31 : 10, 30

IT must have been just about dark, when Ruth, carrying her precious bundle, stepped out of the star-spangled gloaming into the soft light of the oil lamp. Naomi was sitting there, quietly waiting the outcome of day. At the sound of Ruth's foot-steps, she rose to greet her. She had felt keenly for her young daughter-in-law, as she went out in the early morning to try and make her way amongst a people she did not know. She could hardly defer getting out her first question. Ruth was tired, as tired as she had been for many a day, that is, not counting the long day's trek from the Jordan. As she let the grain spill out on an open cloth, Naomi looked on in wonder. Her coarse old hands fondled it gratefully. She lifted some up and let it trail through her fingers. Tears filled her eyes. 'The Lord had visited His people.' Once again, she looked on the fruit of the Land. The barley of Bethlehem was sweet to her; as sweet as the things of the Lord to any who turn from their wilfulness.

'And where have you gleaned today?'[1] asked Naomi. Yes, where indeed? So much to show, for so little labour! So great a fullness, in so short a time! It is a question Christians used to ask each other, when the Bible was the Book of their lives. But people hardly ask it any more. Few really glean in the fields of the Word; and many prefer the menus of Moab.

'The man's name with whom I wrought today is Boaz,' answered Ruth. It was the first time that his name had graced

her lips. Its worth to her was still concealed, though soon his
work would make him known. She mentions it in passing now,
a name that would finally charm her for ever. Ruth must have
been a little startled, therefore, when Naomi exclaimed,

'Blessed be he of the Lord, who hath not left off his kindness to the living and the dead. The man[2] is near of kin unto us,
one of our next kinsmen, one who has the right to redeem.'
Elimelech's name was dead. Here was a name that lived. There
was no telling what the man with the living name of Boaz might
do for them, who dwelt as yet in the deathly shade of Elimelech's
transgression. They were like young girls again as they looked
at the grain. A whole ephah of barley. Just to feel it, was
exciting. How like a kinsman! And how like Boaz! Somehow so
changeless through the years. He had always been like that but it
was only now that Naomi confessed it.

'But that's not all,' said Ruth, 'Here's some parched corn!
He gave it to me specially, when I sat in his presence with the
reapers. Just a little of it satisfies. I have brought the rest for
you.'

There was nothing that Boaz gave, they did not share. When
Christ gives to His own, there is always 'enough and to spare'.
He loves to exceed what we ask or think. When He fed five
thousand, together with their families, there were twelve full
baskets over. One each for the disciples who served with Him
that day. By how much more then, does His rich supply exceed
the needs of one poor soul? Had Naomi and Ruth burst forth in
song, the words of John could well have served them. 'And of
his fullness have all we received, and grace for grace.' The kindness of their mutual Lord drew them still closer to each other.
His joy was now their strength. They could go forward.

The harmony of these two women commands our attention.
The term, 'mother-in-law' occurs ten times in The Book of
Ruth, and its counterpart, 'daughter-in-law' occurs seven times.
This human relationship is notoriously difficult and the mother-
in-law has been depicted very largely, either as a tyrannical,
interfering busybody, or else as an object of ridicule. Left to
their own devices, a mother-in-law and her daughter-in-law can
soon be at loggerheads, and families and marriages have been
torn to pieces through failure to rightly handle this dilemma.

There is, of course, the generation gap which has its problems in any setting, but in this relationship, it is charged with the added dynamite of conflicting loyalties. In the leaving and cleaving that makes a marriage authentic, there is bound to be much heartburning. From the earliest days of courtship, a boy will do for his wife-to-be what he would never do for his mother, be it pursuing his studies, or getting his hair cut. As this becomes evident in a host of ways, the seeds of jealousy are easily sown. The love for his mother seems to wane in direct proportion to her natural possessiveness. In some special way, she still wants him but it becomes increasingly clear that he does not want her as he did and resents her telling him what he should do. He is charming to his fiancée but disconcerting and off-handed to his parents, especially if they dare to express their opinions. It is all very disheartening. The mother of the boy feels especially outraged. She feels, I bore him, fed him, nursed him and reared him. We spent our savings on his education and yet after all this, he goes and pours out his affection and attention on someone he has only lately known, and may subsequently regret he met. The usual remark is then forthcoming. 'What a thankless task, bringing up children!'

Meanwhile the girl becomes afraid that she will lose her lover, perhaps the only one she ever had, and who already means so much to her. In her fear and love she becomes at first defensive and then aggressive, as she tries to isolate the one she would marry. It annoys her when her young husband's mother still speaks to him, writes to him, or sends things to him, as if nothing had happened; as if she, his wife, just did not exist. But this is reciprocal, for it annoys the mother that the young wife, her daughter-in-law, should resent her having dealings with her son. It is ridiculous, she feels. After all, he is still my son whatever his age, and a mother is always a mother. Wait till she gets her own children then she'll understand! The fact of the matter is, however, that the young daughter-in-law has not yet got any children, and she will not understand. She has just got a husband and she would not like to think that his mother would have to be the point of reference all the years of their married life. Unchecked, these undercurrents will accelerate and deepen. Visits to the mother-in-law's will be tense and even

painful and provide fuel for long discussions both in the old
home and the new. The gulf will widen. Contact will slowly die.
The man will not want to be rude or unkind to either his mother
or his wife but in most cases he remains nonplussed, as to how
to handle either. The mother-in-law and the daughter-in-law
will both feel it is the other who creates the problem, and why
does there have to be all this trouble. The two families then drift
apart. The mother-in-law feels it is a shame she never sees her
grandchildren. The daughter-in-law feels it is terrible that her
mother-in-law is not interested in her grandchildren. It is a
predicament to be found in varying degrees of intensity in
thousands of families. The solution to these problems lies very
much with the mother-in-law, as the older and maturer woman.
She has been through the whole circumstance herself. She has
married someone else's son, set up a home and had children.
There is a sense, if she will only remember, in which she, herself, has experienced so much of all that her daughter-in-law
now thinks and feels. As the mother-in-law she has a vital role
to play, not so much in lecturing but in the display of right
attitudes, for in attitude, the heart is revealed and if the heart is
right, it is amazing how much can be amicably arranged. If the
mother-in-law however is childish, and pouts and bristles her
way through; if she forgets her own reactions when young;
her love for her son is only love for herself; if she fails to realise
that only in letting him go *completely*, can she ever hope to
regain him on that higher level of manhood, her chances of ever
having the confidence of his wife, or of being the beloved grand-
mother of his children, are exceedingly slender. It is for her to
set the standard of loving attitudes, even if for the present, the
less she be loved. But what about the daughter-in-law, she may
ask. Should she not reciprocate? Yes, she should, but being
young and inexperienced, and coping with the new experiences
and demands of married life, she is not so likely to analyse the
situation and consciously control her attitudes. She is far more
likely to react emotionally and out of instinct, whereas the
mother-in-law has everything on her side to enable her to
comport herself aright. The most disastrous course the mother-
in-law can adopt, is to persist in criticizing her son's wife to his
face, or continue to perpetuate the strained atmosphere by

being mean and demanding on every family issue. It leads to embitterment of life and disillusionment in age. There is first the sense of feeling unwanted and then the dread realisation in widowhood and infirmity that one is not wanted. All that is left then, is the memory of a baby boy, maybe half a century ago, whom she liked to call her own. Perhaps that is where the mistake begins. A human being is never born to be possessed by any other human being. Procreation requires surrender, first of one's self, and in the end, of the child. Perhaps there is an altar for every Isaac, and a resurrection too, if once we let him go.

The laws of life are so inexorable. They cannot be avoided; neither are they overthrown. They are very old. They need to be acknowledged, not ignored. Love is the nature of the one who made them. When we fight the laws, we soon start fighting people; and in the end we fight with God. Love suffereth long and is kind. Love beareth all things. Love believes and in that faith, finds hope. Love endureth *all* things. Love never fails. It takes the love of God in the heart to move with His laws in life. Little wonder the relationship of the mother-in-law and her daughter-in-law is so brittle, especially when entered upon with nothing but mutual antipathies.

Who then is sufficient for these things? We only have to look at Naomi and Ruth, who raised this relationship to its highest plane, to find the answer. Humanly speaking there could so easily have been recrimination. Ruth might have said to Naomi, Your son was never strong. You never let me in to the whole truth, and now after these few brief years, here I am, a young widow, without even a child to show that I have ever been married. Naomi might have turned to Ruth and said, If you had looked after my son as I did, he might have lived to this day. But any bickering of this nature is completely absent. They have a mutual faith in a common Lord, whose kindness has never ceased in life or in death. The experience of His loving, albeit disciplining hand, has welded them together in days of family joy and devastating grief. They are looking away from each other to Him. They are seeking not their own happiness but the happiness of the other. Naomi is planning for Ruth and Ruth is working for Naomi, not out of duty but out of genuine love.

They are submissive to God. There is no self-assertion. It is
His way, not their own, they wish to tread. It is His interest
they wish to serve. Their preference is undoubtedly His will
and purpose for their lives. They are moving together into His
great plan of redemption. They go forward, not as grasping
what they can, but as feasting on the Lord's provision. They
rejoice in all His work on their behalf. He has done such
wondrous things and they are glad.

Nor can we say that the death of their menfolk made this
difficult relationship to thrive, for when Ruth marries Boaz, the
same sweet spirit still prevails. In Boaz, the part of the son-in-
law is beautifully exemplified. His consideration for Ruth is
great, but he never forgets Naomi. His recognition of what they
mean to each other is undoubtedly profound. His impeccable
moral behaviour towards Ruth, gives Naomi absolute confidence
in his handling of her case. His generosity of heart and his gifts
in kind, all show that attitude of love that seeks to give before
receiving. It is the Lord that makes the difference. They let
Him lead them every step of the way. Happiness after all, is not
something we seek for ourselves but that which becomes our
portion, when we seek it for others. It is love's victory.

But where is 'love'? someone might ask. The answer, in that
former day, was in the God of Israel, but since He has visited us,
we can say today, it is in Christ Jesus our Lord. All those I love,
then, I must hold in Jesus. There they are safe. I do not need
to cling to them with fears lest others rob me of them. God
gave them and He takes away. The leaving and the cleaving
are His own design. I must not fight or scourge another, for
my own poor ends; but love them for their own rich blessing;
love them for Jesus' sake, who loves them best of all. And if the
folk I fail to love, I bring to Him in constant prayer, the day will
dawn when I shall see, He loves them just as He loves me. Then
where is bitterness? Love has long patience. Christ waited long
for me. Shall I not wait for others? Love closes the distances
and when it is perfect, casts out our fears.

Thinking of Naomi and Ruth, it is evident that this vital
relationship between them was not allowed to become anaemic.
It was always virile. Love is a living thing. It is strong for every
demand of life. It is stronger than all in the throes of death. It

speaks the truth when some devoid of love refuse to speak at all. In her exuberance, Ruth says something now that needs correction. Love is not passivity. Love is not abstinence from what might offend. Love is responsible. It will dare misunderstanding to gain a real understanding. Love is positive. It takes steps. It is the nature of the God who moves.

Naomi is in no doubt of Ruth's ethnic origin, but suddenly the Spirit of God records, 'And Ruth, *the Moabitess* said . . .' This warns us that something Moabite in character is about to come out and so it does. 'He said unto me,' continues Ruth, 'Thou shalt keep fast by my young men, until they have ended all my harvest.' In the context it is highly improbable that Ruth said this with any wrong intention but that is not the point. What she said was untrue and it revealed what was latent in her nature by birth. We may not always mean a thing, but it can disclose what we are. She was a young widow whose sorrows were passing. She was now thrown in amongst young folk again, and in a festive mood. Some would turn a blind eye at harvest. Boaz had not forbidden her to talk to the young men. They were there to be of help to her and some had already dropped her a sheaf. Would it not be splendid to keep with them through the whole harvest period? Wasn't that the idea? Isn't that in fact what Boaz said? One glance back into the second chapter will show that Boaz said nothing of the kind. He said, 'Abide here fast by my *maidens*'. This was to be her company, and that is how he put it. It is necessary to realise that even a person of pious mind, by reason of their fallen nature can quickly get ideas inverted. Naomi does not make Ruth an offender for a word but firmly turns her thoughts in the right direction. 'It is good, my daughter,' she says, 'that thou go out with his *maidens*, lest in any other field you be molested.' We are never so pure that we cannot be tempted. In this matter Naomi and Boaz are agreed. Ruth might have been resentful but believing Boaz and Naomi had her best interest at heart; she accepts what they say. Where such a confidence exists and all concerned desire the will of God and seek to fulfil it according to His word, it is marvellous what pitfalls and heartbreaks can be avoided.

These were the days of the Judges, when the vast majority

of the people did what was right in their own eyes. It was a
dangerous age for a young believer. Elimelech, old enough to
know better and mature enough for right judgment, was
caught, nevertheless, in the spirit of the age. Ruth, though so
young in her new-found faith, resists where Elimelech, an older
believer, failed. She was enabled to do this, partly by reason of
that intuitive sense that God grants the freshly blessed; and
also, because, as a young person, she listened to the spiritual
counsel of the right older people. Her heart was basically pure,
thus the issues of her life were preserved. For many young
people, today, this approach to faith and marriage is unaccept-
able. That it should be, is one more tragedy. Ruth counted in
history, but few today will count at all. There is no room for
independent thought, if by that is meant, thinking independently
of God. Man was not made for independence. It leads to the
horror of the ultimate loneliness. The one who goes it alone,
will go until he is alone; and that is a lasting constituent of hell.
In view of this, Ruth's final bliss is eloquent indeed.

NOTES

1. Naomi emphasizes more the nature of the work. It was 'gleaning'. Ruth
is more conscious of its exertion. The onlooker sees what is done; the
participator feels the effort expended. First the pressure; then the prize.
2. Note the expression, 'the man'. It becomes their prime mode of reference
when speaking of Boaz. See 2: 19; 2: 20; 3: 3; 4: 8; 4: 16; 4: 18. For
them, there was only one man, Boaz, who had the right to redeem. For
the Christian, there is only one Man '*the Man* Christ Jesus: He alone gives
us hope of redemption. 'Behold, the Man!' said Pilate; and there has
never been another man since. Christ is 'The Last Adam'.

Seventeen

A Means of Contact

> '*Behold, as the eyes of servants look unto the hand of their masters, and as the eyes of a maiden unto the hand of her mistress; so our eyes wait upon the Lord our God, until that He have mercy upon us.*'
>
> Psalm 123: 2
>
> '*Surely I have behaved and quieted myself, as a child that is weaned of his mother: my soul is even as a weaned child.*'
>
> Psalm 131: 2

THE days of the harvest were quite magnificent. The sun shone out of a bright blue sky. The mountains were clear and the voices of the reapers, in the still air of the hill-country, could be heard right up in the town. Sometimes Naomi, busying herself about the home, would stop a moment and being made conscious of the work below, lift up a prayer for her daughter-in-law, who was better to her than seven sons. She, herself, was regaining her strength and putting on weight once more. She no longer looked so old and broken. She was being nourished on the barley and parched corn of Boaz, her kinsman. Ruth loved the fresh mornings and she revelled in Bethlehem. She worked hard, but the simplicity of the life, the friendliness of the people, and most of all, the nearness of God in the mountains, gave her a new zest of life. She loved Naomi dearly, not only as her mother-in-law but as the one who had, in all her weakness, led her to Jehovah. She felt she owed everything to her and was glad to do anything for her. Then too, there were the mealtimes under the awning. She found herself looking forward so eagerly to these occasions. It was almost as if she were fifteen again, and strings long silenced, were trembling once more. She had her thoughts, though she dare not divulge them. At times she

almost forgot what she was doing and her movements became
mechanical, as she gleaned a few ears here, or an odd stalk there.
The grave in Moab sometimes came before her. It was not long
ago, and she did not want to be disloyal to Mahlon's memory.
But then she would think of Boaz and how he passed her the
corn. 'Why should be take knowledge of me,' she kept asking
herself, 'seeing I am a stranger?' And all day long she would
wonder how it could be!

Then, 'Here you are, Ruth!' some burly young peasant would
shout. And she would look up into the mischievous face of a
man more her age. With a grimace full of meaning, a sheaf
would tumble from his fork. She would smile back with appreciation and he would give her a wink. She was thankful for their
kindly way but none of them moved her. It was generally mid-
morning when Boaz came. Then there was only one man in the
field. And soon it was lunchtime. It worried her at first that she
should feel like that. He always brought the same greeting to his
people. Like himself, it did not change. 'The Lord be with you',
he would say, and she found herself answering with the reapers,
'The Lord bless thee.' And the words, she knew, were right
from her heart.

During this period, Naomi sat much alone. The streets were
mostly deserted in the daytime. Other gentry were reaping, and
it meant there were few at the stalls when she went to buy.
Normally, she only purchased their necessities, a few bean-pods
maybe, a little oil to feed the lamp and once, a simple broom to
sweep the house. Today was different. She bought some cloth.
Such folk she met, were mostly of her generation and knew her
well in days gone by. They talked of former days and spoke
of loved ones passed away. She asked them of their children too.
She was not so embarrassed now. They understood. Perhaps
someone would mention Ruth. She had a place in all their
hearts. They were amazed to see just how she cared for Naomi,
and lived amongst them in such virtue. Some of the womenfolk,
who quarrelled with their daughter-in-laws, were truly envious.
'You don't know just how blessed you are!' they would say to
Naomi. 'We think she's marvellous!' But Naomi kept all these
things deep in her heart. It was the kindness of the Lord.

In the quiet hours, Naomi was thinking a way through for

Ruth. It was no good her marrying just anybody around town.
There was the field to think of and the family name. Unless
someone would buy the field, and at the same time marry her
daughter-in-law, the inheritance would lapse. There would be
no descendants to carry it on, and the name of Elimelech must
perish from the earth. It was all so important in the long term.
She was so anxious, too, that Ruth should be happy. She longed
that her children should inherit the patrimony. The amazing
thing was, that all through harvest, Ruth *had* been happy. That
listless look had gone from her eyes, and although she still wore
the garments of widowhood, she wept no more. Instead, there
was a radiance in her face. It had set Naomi wondering at first;
but she thought she knew why. So she weighed the issues and
continued to pray that all she arranged might prove truly of God.
Her needlework, too, began to make progress.

On the last day of reaping, Naomi made sure she had a good
meal waiting for her daughter-in-law. As soon as Ruth crossed
the threshold she served it, and the weary young woman sat
down gladly and began to relax. Naomi waited awhile and then
she began to speak to her. Lovingly she talked, but with unusual
solemnity. Ruth stopped eating and looked at her quizzically.

'Shall I not seek rest for thee,' she began, 'that it may be well
with thee?'

Ruth was quite taken aback. Was she expected to reply, or
was it just a rhetorical question?

'And now is not Boaz of our kindred,' she went on, 'with
whose maidens thou wast?'

Ruth blushed at the mention of the name, and Naomi knew
she had not misjudged. This was the moment.

'And doesn't he start winnowing tonight,' she asked, 'down
on the threshing floor?'

The end of barley and wheat harvest was usually marked by
an open celebration that went on well into the evening. Many
would gather from the town and the surrounding hamlets, and
Boaz himself would be there at the threshing floor in the fields,
to supervise the next stage of the work and to preside over the
proceedings.

Ruth was now a little on edge and did not know what to say.
A certain sense of excitement was rising in her and she was

puzzled to know what the next step might be. The customs of
the Israelites were still something of an enigma to her, thus she
could only wait until Naomi had outlined her plan. Everything
hinged apparently, on the next of kin. That much she understood. It was one of God's miracles, that of all men in Bethlehem,
Boaz should stand in that relationship. As she listened to Naomi,
it became more and more clear that the time had come for the
family claim to be presented. 'None other than Boaz can do it,'
maintained Naomi. 'He is the one to purchase our field and
raise up a posterity.' That being so, thought Ruth, no doubt
Naomi will take everything in hand, and I, as the foreign
daughter-in-law, will fit in to such arrangements as she makes.

Never, however, in her wildest dreams had Ruth envisaged
the means of approach they were now to employ. There was
more in Naomi that she had thought, and faith had made her as
bold as a lion.

'What you must do', continued Naomi in a voice that brooked
no refusal, 'is to wash and anoint yourself, then put on the new
clothes I have prepared for you and go down to the threshing
floor where Boaz is. The suggestion was more significant than
might first appear. It involved the putting off of the clothes of
the widow and deliberately terminating the days of mourning.
It meant, from the widow's standpoint, declaring herself
eligible again for marriage. Up till now, it would seem Ruth had
not done this, but Naomi in her clear-cut counsel was saying,
This is the time to do it. Ruth in her modesty, could have
quailed at the thought of appearing at night on the threshing
floor, even in her work-a-day clothes, but to go down deliberately
dressed as she had never been dressed in Israel, was almost
beyond her. Indeed it would have been, but for her growing
affection for Boaz. Was not this what she wanted, more than
anything else in the world? When love fills the heart, the most
retiring of personalities blends audacity with modesty, and in so
doing, acquires that element of charm, which wins. Ruth
listened but did not demur. She was being told to do what she
really wanted to do, and Naomi's unfolding of the Law gave her
the moral ground on which to act. It was her longed for
opportunity. The impossible was there for faith to claim. Their
kinsman Boaz would not fail.

The threshing floor, in Scripture, is a place where issues are brought to climax. The threshing floor of Ornan sees God's judgment answered in sacrifice. On the threshing floor of Gideon, God's purposes are proved. On the threshing floor of Satan, Simon's faith in Christ is tested. On the threshing floor of God, His wheat is gathered and the tares are burned. It was at the threshing floor of Atad, that all that spoke of Egypt was left behind, and the sons of Jacob carried their father's remains to the resting place of the purchased possession. On the threshing floor of Boaz, everything of Moab, too, would be discarded. Ruth would emerge from that night of decision, another woman. The threshing floor is thus the place, where everything is settled in principle, whatever else might remain to be done. It is there the Lord answers, as David proved.[1] Both God and Satan sift in their time. Satan winnows us to prove we are all chaff; that no grain of God is in us! God winnows us to remove the chaff; that we might be the good seed of the kingdom, and not a tare amongst us. 'The wicked are like the chaff,' says the Psalmist, 'that the wind driveth away'; and the nations that forget God shall be as the swirling husks of the summer threshing floors. But when the Lord sifts His own, He says, 'not the least grain shall fall on the earth'.[2] 'O my threshing, and the corn of my floor: that which I have heard of the Lord of hosts, the God of Israel, have I declared unto you.'[3] God's word should bring us down to the floor, that there, every issue might be threshed, and all outstanding in our lives, resolved.

Naomi is seeking rest for her daughter-in-law, and she knows where to send her. She will get settlement there. 'Wash thyself', she says, 'therefore, and anoint thee, and put thy raiment upon thee, and get thee down to the floor . . .' The prospect of fellowship with our Beloved on issues concerning our relationship should stir us to preparations suited to the occasion. The three actions Naomi suggests help us to know what we should do.

First of all she says, 'Wash thyself!' Christ has already washed us, for He has loosed us from our sins in His own blood; but there is a sense in which we are to wash ourselves. In view of what He has done to release us from the penalty of sin, we must be concerned, now, about the defilement of sin. We are told to cleanse ourselves from every filthiness of the flesh and spirit. We must lay aside every weight and the sin that so easily besets us. We must purify our hearts, as double-minded. Through His substitution for the sinner, He has established a relationship, but through the confession of our sin we continue in his fellowship. We do this by coming to the light, that everything contrary in us may be reproved. We allow the water of the Word of God to come in contact with our flesh. We acknowledge everything leprous about us and dip until we are entirely clean. We must stand in the good of our baptism.[4] Judicial righteousness is necessary, if we are to come to God. Practical righteousness is necessary if we are to go on with God. The first is our spotless standing in Christ. The second our consistency in following Christ. He has made us pure, but He also says, 'Keep thyself pure'. He has made us holy, yet He says, 'Be ye holy'. God's love is in our hearts but He still says, 'Keep yourselves in it'. Because He has fulfilled His responsibility to the Father, on our behalf, we need to fulfil our responsibility to Him, that the Father in all things might be glorified.

Naomi says, 'Anoint thee!' And again it is something Ruth must do. The believer in Christ has an anointing from the Holy One. Historically this looks back to Pentecost; but practically speaking, if the oil of the Spirit is not freshly upon us, we shall fail miserably in our contact with Christ. He has put the Spirit within us, and upon us, but we still need to walk in the Spirit. It is only in the good of this unction that we enter His mind. It is only through the anointing that we can know God's things, or ever make them known.

The final preparation for Ruth was that she should put on her raiment. There is little doubt, that what she had been wearing, not only revealed that she was a widow, but also declared her Moabite origin. We can also conceive how the new clothes would be those worn by Israelites. To don these clothes, was to express outwardly, what had already taken place within. She was putting off the old and putting on the new. She was discarding, as it were, her sackcloth, that she might gird herself with gladness. She was taking up beauty for ashes; the oil of joy for mourning, and the garment of praise for the spirit of heaviness. It speaks of the renewing of the spirit of the mind; the conscious putting on of the new man, which after God is created in righteousness and true holiness. The old man and his deeds were shelved like a snake-skin. She was now resplendent, to use the New Testament counterpart, in bowels of mercies, kindness, humbleness of mind, meekness and long suffering. Both factually and actually, she was a new creature. She is a bride making herself ready. She will come to Boaz 'in raiment of needle work'. And thus prepared she goes down to the floor.

But the threshing floor was not only a place where the kernel was separated from the husk, and the content set apart from that which was merely external, it was also a lowly place, a location where social differences were lost, as master and servant lay side by side, guarding the precious fruits of the earth. Down the years it has been a common practice in Palestine for owners and their households to camp out at the threshing floors in order to prevent theft from the heaps of grain.[5] 'Get thee down to the floor,' said Naomi, but normally it was not a place for a single woman. Ruth was only authorised to go there by reason of the propriety of her plea. She did not appear there contrary to law but rather that the provisions of law might be honoured. She went, not as seducer but as a suppliant; not to prostitute her womanhood but preserve it. She took the lowly place, and faced up to her crisis. She got down to the floor to the feet of her kinsman, and all her problems were answered there.

It reminds us of another woman who came to the Lord Jesus and took up a similar position. Of her it is written, 'She stood at His feet . . . she washed His feet . . . she wiped His feet . . . she kissed His feet . . . she anointed His feet.' 'Thou gavest me no kiss,' Jesus says to the Pharisee, '. . . but this woman since . . . I came in hath not ceased to kiss my feet.' Eve, the first woman, tried to be the head. She swayed the First Man; but how blessed the woman, who in humility and contrition places her head at the feet of the Second Man. Boaz is the second man for Ruth. Mahlon, her first man, was a 'fallen' man; the grave had claimed him. He could not lead her anywhere or do anything for her. But Boaz, her second man, lived. He would bring her into all the inheritance of God. Ruth had found grace. Now she advanced in grace. First his gift, and then her growth. She had gleaned in his field; now she must kneel on his floor. Many are they who do the first but few are they who do the latter. In the field I gather; but on the floor I give myself away.

> *Enough O Lord, Thy conquest is complete.*
> *Thy love foreknew, yet bore all shame for me.*
> *Mine outpoured soul shall lave Thy piercéd feet.*
> *Thy great forgiveness bind my soul to Thee.*[6]

NOTES

1. I Chronicles 21 : 28
2. Amos 9 : 9
3. Isaiah 21 : 10
4. Acts 22 : 16 with Romans 6 : 6
5. The threshing floor at this period in Israel was not normally located in a barn but a smooth area of hard sun-baked mud specially made for the occasion in the midst of the fields.
6. Part of a poem composed by the author whilst in solitary confinement, as a prisoner, in Red China.

Eighteen

The Daring Claim

> *'In whom also we have obtained an inheritance, being*
> *predestinated according to the purpose of Him who*
> *worketh all things after the counsel of His own will.'*
>
> Ephesians 1: 11

As they ate together, Naomi discussed her plan in greater detail.
Having told Ruth of the preparations she was to make, and the
place she was to occupy, she now tells her when she is to act. In
all our communion there is the manner, the place and the time.
To disregard any of these aspects can cause loss in our approaches to our Master. The time for her to draw near to Boaz
and disclose her identity was 'when he had done eating and
drinking'. One hesitates to weight the narrative with overmuch
application, but there came a moment prior to the cross, when
our Lord had also done eating and drinking. In Luke, Jesus
says, 'With desire I have desired to eat this passover with you
before I suffer for I say unto you, I will not any more eat there-
of, until it be fulfilled in the Kingdom of God.' Then in
Matthew, Jesus says, 'I say unto you, I will not drink hence-
forth of this fruit of the vine, until that day when I drink it
new with you in my Father's Kingdom.' He was coming to 'the
midnight hour' of Calvary, with all its horror. He had, therefore, done with both eating and drinking. He was going there to
secure His harvest. It was God's threshing floor in the midst of
the years, where the issues of grace and judgment would be
brought to climax.

If we wish to approach Him, our kinsman of flesh and blood,
then, like the Jewish thief and the Gentile centurion, we must
meet Him there. Though aliens to God, they knew their time.
They did not miss it. The Son of Man had come eating and
drinking, but all that was over. Now He was Himself the Bread,

and His own blood the Wine. To eat of the multiplied loaves and
fishes, afforded a physical experience, charged with miracle,
but to eat of His flesh and drink of His blood, meant to assimi-
late by faith the very essence of Christ. It is the true appropria-
tion of the Son, and this is Life. Once we partake of Him, we,
too, will have done eating and drinking. We shall never hunger,
and we shall never thirst. Ruth had eaten of Boaz's bread, now
she would go to Boaz in person. At His feet was her place; and
this was the time. He would not disappoint her. He would
satisfy her heart.

'He will lie down,' continued Naomi. It brought to mind her
childhood days, when, before the famine, she and her parents
slept out of doors beside the grain. 'And when he does,' she
went on, 'thou shalt mark the place where he shall lie, and thou
shalt go in, and uncover his feet.' We think of the words in
Luke when 'the women . . . beheld the sepulchre, and how his
body was laid.' They watched in grief; but what a change, when
the first-day-sunshine flooded the tomb. 'Come, see the place
where the Lord lay,' said the angels in Matthew; and 'Behold
the place where they laid Him,' in the Gospel by Mark. Jesus
had lain in death but had risen in life.

Ruth, it has been said, and it is very true, was identified with
Boaz in his lying down and his rising up. 'When he lay down, she
lay down. When he rose up, she rose up.' She was so changed by
her experience on the threshing floor that on her return, Naomi
was constrained to ask her, 'Who art thou, my daughter?'
Whoever is identified with Christ in his lying down in death and
rising up in life, is always radically changed. Ruth came forth
from this encounter, ready to yield herself completely to Boaz.
In like manner, the believer, thus identified with Christ, comes
forth from the night to yield his members unto holiness and
bear fruit unto God.

After noting the place where Boaz lay, Ruth was to enter the
circle of sleeping retainers and uncover his feet; the feet of him
who had walked out from Bethlehem to the floor in the hills.
It speaks of the path that our Saviour trod. His feet were first
uncovered, when John perceived Him at the river. The dove
descending marked Him out. John looked on Jesus as He walked
and then proclaimed, 'Behold the Lamb . . .!' His feet revealed

His great direction. And where were they going, those feet of the Master? They were going to Calvary, the Floor in the hills, that place of the ploughing, the sowing and reaping, where the Grain was secured.[1]

The paths of His feet are peace to His followers, and all His footsteps sow light in the way. He walks by the sea and He walks on the sea, the Lord of the calm and the Lord of the storm. He walks straight through, doing His good; then walks no more in Jewry. He walks in Solomon's porch, a pillar greater than Boaz, and a king greater than Solomon. Then he walks where Solomon never walked, up Calvary's mountain. It is His third day march and he walks to a finish. 'They pierced my hands and my feet,' He says; and many would doubt of His walking again. But He walked right through them and went His way. He stripped off from Him the hostile princes. He made them His conquests. All through the valley of the shadow He walked. He filled it with light; then into the dawn, from the grave He had plundered. He walked with His own on the road to Emmaus. Their hearts were burning. Their tears were dried. He stood in the midst of His frightened disciples. 'Behold . . . my feet,' He said; and there they uncovered them. They were beautiful feet. They were full of good tidings, feet with wounds, yet feet of flame. Feet of suffering and feet of glory. Feet treading down shame!

At present the night is still with us, and like Ruth, we can only uncover the feet of our Kinsman, and mark where He lay. 'We see not yet all things put under Him but in the morning, He will come to us and load us afresh with His benefits, just as Boaz did Ruth. Then we shall see His face, the face of Him, whose feet we looked on in the night.

Naomi's final instruction to Ruth was, that having uncovered the feet of her kinsman, she should then lie down discreetly and await his word. That is where Mary found her place, at the feet of her Lord. Hers was the portion that Jesus called 'good'. It was granted from God and it would not be lost. Good things are hardly gained and easily squandered. It is only at the Redeemer's feet that good things once obtained, can also be retained. Such is the blessing of the Lord. 'It maketh rich and addeth no sorrow with it.'

'He will tell thee', declared Naomi, 'what thou shalt do.' One needs patience to await directives, especially in the dark. Saul of Tarsus, a desperately active man, asks, on his encounter with Jesus Christ, 'Lord, what wilt Thou have me to do?' But he is not immediately informed. 'Go into the city,' says the Lord Jesus, 'and it shall be told thee what thou must do.' The vision may tarry; but it is imperative to wait for it.

Then Ruth replied, to Naomi, 'All that thou sayest unto me I will do.' And away she went to make herself ready.

NOTES

1. Cf. Amos 9: 13. As at the Cross, so in the Kingdom, all these processes come together. 'Behold, the days come, saith the Lord, that the plowman shall overtake the reaper . . .'.

Nineteen

A Woman at Midnight

*'Blessed be the Name of God for ever and ever: for . . .
He revealeth the deep and secret things: He knoweth
what is in the darkness, and the light dwelleth with
Him.'*

Daniel 2 : 20–22

NAOMI had never doubted the beauty of Ruth but now, as she
stood in the lamplight, in a simple, but spotless Hebrew dress
ready for her great adventure, Naomi thought the world of her.
She watched her take her way through the darkened street, the
outlines of the houses etched in silver, by the harvest moon.
There were bonfires in the fields below the terraces, and by
their friendly glare, Ruth picked out her path. Others were going
too. There would be singing and dancing, sweetmeats and wine.
It was a time of rejoicing for the ingathered harvest. After the
long weeks of labour, this was a welcome break and the local
peasantry entered with zest into the few hours festivities. Ruth
mingled with the crowds thronging the newly cut fields. The
stubble was coarse under foot, something she barely noticed in
the daytime. She watched the swaying figures, men and girls,
stepping first forwards and then backwards, their faces aglow
with the firelight. Their songs told of the mercy of the Lord.
One would soliloquize on some aspect of His goodness, and then
in chorus, a host of voices would ring out in response. It struck
Ruth as all so carefree, and void of superstition, at least in the
fields of Boaz. There were no sticks of incense burning in the
earth, and no idols esconced there under the stars, carried out
for the occasion from some filthy temple. The Lord was with
the reapers in their joy and leisure, just as He had been through
all the weeks of work. There was something infectious about it
all. This was Israel. Moab was strangely far away and Ruth
was glad to have it so.

The evening lengthened. Those with children tended to disperse. The fourth gong after sunset sounded. The ranks of dancers gradually diminished. Ruth lingered on. She had seen Boaz at some distance, looking contentedly on the happiness of his people, but she had not, as yet, ventured to approach the threshing floor or the awning beside it. The fifth gong sounded. Quite a number of the young folk still stood talking and laughing. The hour was late. The steward came over. He cautioned them and they withdrew to their homes in the village, or their encampments at the edge of the field. The fires subsided, till all Ruth could see, was here and there a sullen redness in the night. By the heaps of grain, someone poked the embers, and for a few brief minutes, the dying flames permitted her to see where Boaz and his men reclined. Silence descended on the deserted field. Only the hooting of an owl and the faint moan of the night breeze fell on her ears. She stepped a little nearer. Now she could hear their breathing. They were heavy with sleep. She halted. A servant rose and put more wood upon the fire. Things grew brighter, but in the gloom she was not seen. She waited several minutes, till no one stirred. Quietly she slipped through the circle of sleepers. She reached him, but her heart was pounding. What was she doing? Her confidence was in the word of Naomi, who loved Jehovah. She knew the Law. By that authority alone she acted. God would not fail her. She lay down on the floor at the feet of her kinsman. She could not see his face in the darkness, but she took no liberties. She must behave. She must be what she was expected to be; and do what she was expected to do. Only God could bestow what she needed. No carnal hand could claim the redeemer. The fire died down and she could hardly perceive him. But his form was there. She felt for his homespun gown which served as a blanket. It was fine to the touch, woven throughout and of beautiful texture. She tugged it a little, then eased it away. She uncovered his feet, but did not touch them. Sufficient for her that they were his, and she was there. 'Would they stand on Elimelech's soil;' she asked herself; 'and lead her onward through the years?' The man stirred uneasily at the movement. It was midnight. Startled from sleep, he sat upright. The fire flickered. What had awakened him? He discerned the shadowy mounds of grain, and the twinkling stars below the awning. Then he looked at his feet. There was someone there. A sense of fear laid hold on him. He glimpsed the profile. It was a woman!

'Who are you!' he exclaimed with bated breath, but in a voice that demanded an answer. This was an impossible intrusion, and he was trembling.

'I am Ruth,' came back the answer. Her quiet word and the alien accent gave it validity. Her name thus spoken, recalled for him her gracious presence in the field. How he had watched her, and asked concerning her! In one sense he had everything; so much to share, but never a bride. Many respected him; but who loved him? He was older now. The years were passing. Rahab his mother had been wonderful, so greathearted in Israel. She had tasted grace and had taught it too, but some would say how she came from Jericho. It always hurt him. He was good enough as an employer, and good enough in the gate, but not quite good enough, it would seem, for anyone's daughter. It had not embittered him, but his longing remained.

'I am Ruth', the young one was saying, 'thine handmaid.'[1] The force of the words dawned slowly on his drowsy mind. 'I am Ruth . . . I am thine . . .,' she was saying. 'Spread therefore thy skirt over me; for thou art a near kinsman.' It was *his* term she had adopted, the word he had used for the wings of Jehovah. Beneath His feathers she had trusted. 'Spread thy wing over me,' she was asking now . . .[2]

Boaz, sitting there, beneath the awning, senses the coolness on his feet. He thinks of the lateness of the hour and the serious hazard of Ruth's undertaking. He is deeply moved. He could not have believed she would accord to him this opportunity, or go to such lengths to proffer it. After all, she was a Moabitess; she was young; and had known already the experience of married life. She could have taken up with someone else so readily. Knowing of God's kindness to his Gentile mother, he had shewn his care for Ruth as a stranger in his gates. It had touched him to think on her care towards Naomi, but here was a kindness that excelled all other.

'Blessed be thou of the Lord, my daughter:' he whispers, 'for thou hast showed more kindness in the latter end than at the beginning, inasmuch as thou followedst not young men,

whether poor or rich.' Ruth listens intently to what he says;
but is anxious for more. She waits for that word which will alter
everything. He does not delay, for Boaz means 'fleetness' as well
as 'ability'. He speaks at once. 'And now my daughter, fear not;'
he says. 'I will do to thee all that thou requirest: for all the city
of my people doth know thee, as a "bride worth the winning".'³
The bliss of that moment would be with her always. She felt so
impotent, but the kinsman she loved would do everything for
her. It was enough. Now he had pledged himself. All would be
well.

She must know, however, the exact position. There was
another kinsman and he must be contacted. As a nearer
relation, he might handle the matter. 'But in his default' said
Boaz, and he seemed to foresee it, 'I will do for thee, the
kinsman's part.' With those words ringing in her heart, 'I
will do all . . . I will do the kinsman's part,' Ruth at the behest
of Boaz, lies down until the morning. She does not fret. The
redeemer has spoken. How sweet to rest in the promise he gives.

All this emphasises the nature of the midnight scenes in
Scripture. Midnight is the hour of both doom and salvation.
How safe and strong is the one who trusts in God, at this
mysterious moment of life and death. It was at midnight that
the Destroyer passed through Egypt and the Lord in protecting
grace hovered over His own, sheltered by the blood of the lamb.⁴
It was at midnight, that Samson unhinged the doors of the gates
of Gaza and shouldered them twenty miles to the hills of
Hebron. It was at midnight that Paul and Silas prayed and sang,
till the earth was shaken and the jailer converted. It was at
midnight, in the parable, that the bridegroom came to receive
his bride and the five wise virgins entered in. Ruth at midnight
had a foretaste of all this. 'I will do all . . .' declares Boaz. 'I will
do the kinsman's part.'

With strictest propriety, Ruth lay where she was, but at the
first light of dawn, Boaz was up, and as he arose, Ruth rose
also. They had done honour to each other. Their good must not
be evil spoken of. 'Let it not be known', he says, 'that a woman
came into the floor.' As she is about to leave, Boaz leads her
over to a heap of barley. He notices her change of clothing and
his heart is quickened. 'Bring the vail thou hast upon thee,' he

tells her. The word means 'a covering' and perhaps in part was concealing her face. She removes it as desired and they look into each other's eyes. In the night it was his feet but now, 'face to face'. There is nothing between. 'Hold the vail in your hands,' says Boaz. Then one by one he counts each measure. What kind is left unmentioned. It is the number that matters. There are six all together. The light fills up his countenance as he pours her out the golden grain. 'You must not go empty-handed,' he says. 'Take this to your mother-in-law.' Together, they make 'a sack' of the mantle and he lifts it to her back. His eyes look longingly after her, as she crosses the fields and makes her way up to the city in the dawn . . . Yes it was 'a night to be remembered', and hers, a courage to be revered. Today he would have business in the gate, the transaction of a lifetime.

When Ruth did not return by the fifth gong after sunset, Naomi concluded that Ruth had ventured, as she had told her. It was a long, slow night for Naomi and she was up much earlier than usual. All the time she was wondering how things had gone. She would like to have looked down the road to the fields, but the neighbours might wonder what she was doing at that hour in the morning; and the last thing she wanted was to compromise Ruth's character. As it was, before anyone had time to greet another, Ruth came in, carrying her barley.

'Well, who are you now, my daughter?' was Naomi's greeting. It was a significant question. The events of the night could make her another's ere the day was out. Together they sat down and Ruth poured forth her story. Naomi could have wept for her, as 'she told her all that the man had done unto her'. Every detail brought its own joy. Once all Naomi's questions were answered, they turned together to the grain. 'Boaz gave me six measures,' Ruth said, 'and he told me they were specially for you.'

'You were sure there were six,' asked Naomi, inquisitively.

'No more and no less,' replied Ruth. 'He counted them out most carefully.' To Naomi this was more than a gift. It was a sign. Was it not six days the Creator took to make the world; and only when His work was done, He chose to rest?

'Six measures,' mused Naomi pensively. 'He's going through with it, Ruth, there is no doubt about it! So sit still, my daughter, until thou know how the matter will fall: for the man will not be in rest, until he have finished the thing this day.'

NOTES

1. Ruth used another word earlier, when speaking of the handmaidens of Boaz, which viewed them as higher than herself on the social scale. Ruth employs a Hebrew word here, which is translated 'bond woman', when used of Hagar in Genesis chapter 21. She takes the place of a female slave and this is borne out, for the Greek paidiskē is used for Hagar in Galatians 4 and conveys, of course, the identical idea. See 2 : 13; and then 3 : 9 with Gen. 21 : 10 and Gal. 4 : 30.
2. The spiritual force of this is demonstrated in Ezekiel 16 : 8. 'I looked upon thee . . . I spread my skirt over thee . . . I sware unto thee . . . I entered into a covenant with thee, saith the Lord God, and thou becamest mine.' Similar custom prevailed amongst the Arabs, the descendants of Ishmael. The practice looks back, therefore, to a common origin in patriarchal times, when marriage and kinship went hand in hand. See Abraham's charge to his servant concerning a bride for Isaac. Genesis 24 : 1–6.
3. Knox's expression for 'a virtuous woman' in this particular context.
4. In Exodus 12 : 12–13, there are, of course, two different Hebrew words for the English 'pass'; the 'passing through' (abar); and 'the passing' or 'hovering over' (pasach). It is from the second, that the word 'paschal' comes, but our word 'pass-over' hardly conveys its meaning.

AN HOUR AT THE GATE

Then went Boaz up to the gate, and sat him down there: and behold: the kinsman of whom Boaz spake came by; unto whom he said, Ho, such a one! turn aside, sit down here. And he turned aside, and sat down.

And he took ten men of the elders of the city, and said, Sit ye down here. And they sat down.

And he said unto his kinsman, Naomi, that is come again out of the country of Moab, selleth a parcel of land, which was our brother Elimelech's:

And I thought to advertise thee, saying, Buy it before the inhabitants and before the elders of my people. If thou wilt redeem it, redeem it: but if thou wilt not redeem it, then tell me, that I may know: for there is none to redeem it beside thee; and I am after thee. And he said, I will redeem it.

Then said Boaz, What day thou buyest the field of the hand of Naomi, thou must buy it also of Ruth the Moabitess, the wife of the dead, to raise up the name of the dead upon his inheritance.

And the kinsman said, I cannot redeem it for myself, lest I mar mine own inheritance: redeem thou my right to thyself; for I cannot redeem it.

Now this was the manner in former time in Israel concerning redeeming and concerning changing, for to confirm all things; a man plucked off his shoe, and gave it to his neighbour: and this was a testimony in Israel.

Therefore the kinsman said unto Boaz, Buy it for thee. So he drew off his shoe.

And Boaz said unto the elders, and unto all the people, Ye are witnesses this day, that I have bought all that was Elimelech's, and all that was Chilion's and Mahlon's, of the hand of Naomi.

Moreover Ruth the Moabitess, the wife of Mahlon, have I purchased to be my wife, to raise up the name of the dead upon his inheritance, that the name of the dead be not cut off from among his brethren and from the gate of his place: ye are witnesses this day.

And all the people that were in the gate, and the elders, said, We are witnesses. The Lord make the woman that is come into thine house like Rachel and like Leah, which two did build the house of Israel: and do thou worthily in Ephratah, and be famous in Bethlehem:

And let thy house be like the house of Pharez, whom Tamar bare unto Judah, of the seed which the Lord shall give thee of this young woman.

So Boaz took Ruth, and she was his wife: and when he went in unto her, the Lord gave her conception, and she bare a son.

And the women said unto Naomi, Blessed be the Lord, which hath not left thee this day without a kinsman, that his name may be famous in Israel.

And he shall be unto thee a restorer of thy life, and a nourisher of thine old age: for thy daughter in law, which loveth thee, which is better to thee than seven sons, hath born him.

And Naomi took the child, and laid it in her bosom, and became nurse unto it.

And the women her neighbours gave it a name, saying, There is a son born to Naomi; and they called his name Obed: he is the father of Jesse, the father of David.

Now these are the generations of Pharez: Pharez begat Hezron,

And Hezron begat Ram, and Ram begat Amminadab,

And Amminadab begat Nahshon, and Nahshon begat Salmon,

And Salmon begat Boaz, and Boaz begat Obed,

And Obed begat Jesse, and Jesse begat David.

Twenty

The Gate of His Place

*'There remaineth therefore a rest to the people of God.
For he that is entered into his rest, he also hath ceased
from his own works, as God did from his.'*
Hebrews 4: 9, 10
'The well of Bethlehem, which is by the gate.'
II Samuel 23: 15

'THE sleep of a labouring man is sweet,' writes the Preacher,
and in so doing, sums up the Biblical doctrine of rest. God
always rests in a finished work. When all is done and pro-
nounced very good, He enters upon His sabbath. There are
three words for 'rest' in The Book of Ruth. The first one is
'menuchah', 'a place to dwell'. It was used by Naomi in the first
chapter, when she said to Ruth and Orpah, 'The Lord grant you
that ye may find rest, each of you in the house of her husband.'
Naomi then insisted it was *their own* concern. But there was no
rest in Moab. It spoke of their past and things natural. There
was no rest in the flesh, and no future either; no solution for
tragic dilemma. But in chapter three, Naomi makes Ruth's
rest *her* concern. 'Shall I not seek rest for thee, that it may be
well with thee?' The word here is 'manoach'. It means 'a place
to stand' and was used of the dove when it found no rest and
returned to the ark, the only place for its feet in a world stricken
by judgment. Naomi had progressed greatly in her aspirations
for her daughter-in-law. She was concerned now, not so much
with an abode or place of shelter, which might be anywhere,
but she wanted a standing for her in Israel. It is only when a
person has a standing before God and a portion with the
redeemed, that there is rest for his soul. The third mention of
'rest' is at the close of the third chapter. And here Naomi makes
it the concern of the kinsman. It is *his* concern. 'The man will

not be in rest,' she says, 'until he have finished the thing this day.' This word is 'shaqat', and means 'a state of quietness'. The last words of Boaz in the story can be summed up in the expression, 'I have bought all . . . ye are witnesses'. Then he is quiet. The work is done. He is at rest and Ruth is his. All the rest of Ruth, from that moment on, was in the rest that Boaz secured through the price of redemption. The Law was satisfied. He was satisfied. Now Ruth was satisfied. She had rest in all its aspects; an abode, a standing, and a place of quietness under the wing of her kinsman redeemer, God's man.

It turns our eyes to the cross of Christ, where our Saviour cried with a loud voice, 'It is finished'. Then He is quiet. He says no more save in committal. He could rest in a finished work. Like Ruth, when our Redeemer accomplishes all things for us, we can sit still and rest in what He does. We cease from our own works. His rest is our rest, a rest that remains. Ruth could make nothing of herself, her nature or her background. She had no part in the act of redemption. As she takes her place alongside Boaz, she can only say with Paul and many others down the succeeding years, 'By the grace of God I am what I am'. For we also 'have access by faith into this grace wherein we stand, and rejoice in the hope of the glory of God'.

Naomi is right in her assessment of Boaz. With the swiftness that his name implies, he goes to work. God is slow to anger but swift to bless and those who love Him act most like Him. The settlement of the question becomes paramount. Necessity is laid upon him. 'He must needs go through . . .' 'He must work whilst it is day.' He must complete what he has set out to do. His whole approach to the task, and the spirit in which he performs it, leads us to Christ. 'I must . . .' 'I must . . .' The compulsion of love leads the kinsman on till all is finished, the bride is won, and the inheritance secured.

The attitude of Naomi in all this is noteworthy. In Leviticus twenty-five and Deuteronomy twenty-five, the teaching of the Law is quite plain. On the death of a husband in Israel, his property was to go to his eldest son, rather than the widow. Following Elimelech's decease, therefore, Mahlon acquired the first claim. In the case of two brothers, the elder boy must get two thirds and the younger one third. Orpah, maintaining her

Moabite position as she did, had forfeited any claim through
Chilion. She remained by choice, an alien to the commonwealth
of Israel. Consequently, Ruth as the widow of the elder son was
potential claimant under the Law to the entire estate, providing
the next of kin would marry her and raise up seed to possess it.
By this practice, not only could the inheritance be retained
within the family, but children be born who could possess it,
enjoy it, and carry on the name of their forebears.

Had Naomi acted in mere selfish interest and disregarded the
finer points of the law, she might have said to Ruth, 'Look, we
are short of money. Elimelech was my husband and he and I
owned this piece of land. It's all very well to talk about your
having a stake in it, but I am just going to sell it and realise what
I can.' In this way the whole inheritance would have passed
from Elimelech's posterity and his name would have been cut
off in Israel. This would not do. Orpah was an unbeliever and
Ruth was a new believer; but Naomi was a restored believer
and as such had her special zeal for God. She had gone out
contrary to the Word of God, but now she was back in the Land
she would submit to the Word of God. The man who bought
the field must marry Ruth. The next of kin must answer to his
legal obligation. There was no other way to blessing. Only in
ordering their affairs by the Word of God would they go forward in the will of God. If she had realised this earlier, she
could have had rest at the beginning of her way as well as at the
end. She had learned much by bitter experience. All she wanted
now, was for Ruth to find her rest according to the mind of God.
She had bought the truth at fearful cost. She would not sell it
for mere cash in hand. Her love was growing to perfection. She
would not seek her own but another's wealth. She had no fears.

Now that the harvest was over the streets were crowded.
Every one was out doing the shopping they had hoped to do, as
soon as they were paid and had time to do it. It must have been
about mid-morning, when Boaz made his way through the busy
main streets of Bethlehem and sat down in the gate. There was a
constant coming and going. Donkeys and mules, weighed down
with their loads, were on their way from the caravanseries to
outlying parts. Women, upright as palm trees, carried their
water-pots from the nearby well. Scribes sat in the shadow of

the old stone archway, writing letters and noting transactions for the illiterate. There was a brisk market in all kinds of fruit. Sacks of grain were being auctioned down the street; and the approaches to the city were cluttered with all sorts of folk sitting with baskets and selling a variety of wares. They shouted and haggled, lost their tempers, laughed raucously, hissed for customers[1] and clapped their hands. Everywhere underfoot, was foul smelling garbage. Here and there beggars rummaged hopefully for food. Ragged, but bright-eyed peasants, sported their recent earnings. There was barter and coin. Amongst the crowd, there also walked well-dressed Levites in their priestly habit, wealthy farmers, and merchants, trailed by grubby urchins pleading their favour. Most pathetic of all were the blind and maimed at their daily stance, each shouting aloud to the passers-by; but there was hope for their bowls on this day of plenty, for the harvest was in and soon it was Pentecost.

Boaz eyed them all with a purpose. He was seeking one man. Suddenly out rang his greeting to the person he wanted. He turned abruptly to see what was happening. 'Come and sit down here,' said Boaz. The man obeyed, quite obviously ignorant of the point in question. Although a nearer relation than Boaz, Naomi had never approached him, nor had he sought her, since her return. There seemed a distance. Either the man was devoid of interest or wilfully incognito. Whatever the reason, Boaz now broached the issue in hand.

In the gate all matters of moment were decided. The gates of Israel's cities were meant to be the 'gates of righteousness'; gates of which it could be said, 'The Lord loveth the gates of Zion'. There the law suits were decided. Beneath its arches the elders sat in solemn conclave. To turn aside the poor in the gate was an abomination to the Lord; for it was the bounden duty of the authorities 'to hate evil, love good and establish judgment in the gate'. There, the standards of the Great King were to be upheld, for 'He ruleth over all'. Not only in the millenial day but in all generations, the governors of a city should be able to say, 'Lift up your heads, O ye gates ... and the King of Glory shall come in'. The gate on the other hand could be a place of perversion, as with Absalom who stole the hearts of the people there. It could be a place of shame, as when

Joab slew Abner at the gate of a city of refuge. It could be a place of retribution, as when Jehu made pronouncement on the heads of Ahab's seventy sons. It was a place of execution, for Christ also suffered without the gate, numbered with the transgressors. Primarily, however, the gates of a city were to be the seat of righteousness. 'Speak ye every man truth to his neighbour,' said Zechariah in a later day, 'execute the judgment of truth and peace in your gates.'

Boaz was one of those, in Bethlehem, who maintained these principles in the seat of authority. He had gone up to the gate and sat down. He was there to show grace, but he would do it only on the ground of righteousness. Grace without righteousness is only specious favour. Christ who died for us without the gate, sits today in the Gate of Heaven. He is there with all authority, sat down in His Father's Throne. He is there to show grace, but it is only because He has met the claims of Law. The Throne of Grace and the Righteous Sceptre are indivisible in the affairs of God. Christ has sat down, having by Himself purged our sins. That was the price and having paid it, He has brought us in and brought us nigh. Divine grace when it reigns, can only do so through divine righteousness, but once it reigns, it proclaims eternal life to all who believe.

Boaz exemplifies this, as he calls together ten elders of the city. They are there as representing the Law. They witness to it. They insist on its claims and testify that they have been met. If we think of the decalogue as the epitome of the Law, then these ten men are illustrative of it. The numeral 'ten' in Scripture emphasises man's responsibility.[2] If there had been ten righteous men in Sodom, God would have spared it. The prominence of the figure ten in the measurements of the tabernacle, the temple of Solomon and the temple in Ezekiel are indicative of man's responsibilities before God in all his service. To this, nature adds its witness, with our ten fingers and ten toes, emphasising our responsibility in all our work and in all our walk. Daniel and his colleagues said to the prince of the eunuchs in Babylon, 'Prove thy servants, I beseech thee, ten days'. The Spirit, likewise, says to the church at Smyrna, 'Behold, the devil shall cast some of you into prison, that ye may be tried; and ye shall have tribulation ten days: be thou

faithful unto death, and I will give thee a crown of life.' 'Ten
days' was the symbolical, if not literal period, in which God's
people in this harrowing trial, must show themselves His
responsible witnesses. It took, as previously noted, ten generations of a Moabite family to prove themselves worthy in the
things of Jehovah. And it is interesting to note also in the
Book of Ruth that it took ten years before Naomi acted responsibly and came back to Bethlehem. If Mahlon had married very
young in Moab, and Ruth's espousal to the son of a Hebrew
family was taken as public alignment with their faith, then it
was at least ten years she had been officially, if not spiritually,
connected with Israel. Be this as it may, the presence of ten
men especially constituted as witnesses is evidence of the high
sense of responsibility with which Boaz entered upon this
transaction. The outcome was that once Boaz had completed
the transaction, not one of them could raise an accusing finger
to invalidate what was done. Indeed, should any other party
seek to cast doubt on the transaction of that day, these very
witnesses would be there to uphold it.

It emphasises the glorious doctrines of grace. Christ is the
end of the Law to all who believe. 'Who shall condemn us
now?' cries Paul. 'Who shall lay anything to the charge of God's
elect?' Christ our heavenly Boaz fulfilled the Law and made it
honourable. He was a minister of the circumcision for the truth
of God. He brought out the weightier matters of the Law,
namely, justice, mercy and faith. He revealed its inward spirit
and its historical function. He lived it out in life and met its
claims in death. What the Law demanded, grace provided.
Thus the Law upheld and honoured grace, because it was
extended to the sinner, in complete accord with its requirements. There was nothing left outstanding. There were no
loose ends; no loop holes for the devil to exploit. It was precisely along these lines that Boaz operated. He would show
grace, but he would do it absolutely according to Law. Only
thus could he forge a relationship with Ruth that could not be
dissolved. The case was settled and the ten assembled elders
wholly satisfied in every detail. It was completely authentic.

Truly it could be said of Ruth's husband, 'He is known in the
gates, when he sitteth among the elders of the land,'[3] for was she

not also a virtuous woman. When Solomon described such a woman and her spouse, could it be he had Ruth and Boaz in mind. After all the child they bore of such a union was his own great grandfather!

NOTES

1. E.g., Isaiah 5 : 26 and Ezekiel 27 : 36
2. The Jews seem to recognise this principle as ten persons were deemed necessary for the formation of a synagogue.
3. Proverbs 31

Twenty-one

A Shoe on the Wrong Foot

> 'What? know ye not that your body is the temple of the
> Holy Ghost which is in you, which ye have of God,
> and ye are not your own? For ye are bought with a
> price: therefore glorify God in your body . . .'
>
> I Corinthians 6: 19, 20
>
> 'Christ also loved the church, and gave Himself for
> it . . . That He might present it to Himself . . .'
>
> Ephesians 5: 25–27

THE shout of Boaz to his unnamed kinsman must have aston-
ished not a few. People were used to seeing Boaz, and responded
daily to his greetings. Those that worked for him would be
familiar with his courteous speech but they were not accustomed
to his shout. He did not strive with men or cry aloud; nor was
his voice heard in the streets. But today was different. He would
send forth judgment unto victory and in his name would a
Gentile trust. Balaam, although instructed to curse Israel, had
to say, 'The Lord His God is with him, and the shout of a king
is among them!' 'Ho, such a one!' calls Boaz. The expression
does not lose decorum. The kingly line is in formation. The cry
is princely.

We do not think of shouting when we talk of Deity, but 'the
Lord is like a mighty man that shouteth' says the Scripture, for
all His works of grace and power go forth with a shout. His
voice is that which breaks the cedars; before Him proud men
bow. It makes the hinds to calve; the trembling soul brings
forth for God. When Jesus died, he died with a shout. 'When I
cry and shout,' says the weeping prophet, 'He shutteth out my
prayer.'[1] With a loud voice, his anguish poured forth. 'My God,
my God, why hast thou forsaken me?' With a loud voice, He
gave up the ghost. The attention of heaven, of earth and of hell;

the ears of the Father, of demons and of men, all register the triumph of that shout. 'It is finished!' He cries. O what shoutings from the tree! Their echo will reverberate like the roaring of innumerable cataracts through all the ageless infinitudes of the new heaven and the new earth, for God was in Christ reconciling the world unto Himself. They will be part of the very atmosphere of bliss and torment. We see Him ascend and we exult 'God has gone up with a shout, the Lord with the sound of a trumpet'. Now is the day of The Jubilee come. His blood has been shed and atonement accomplished. The Gospel trumpet proclaims His liberty to helpless slaves and hopeless debtors. Redemption was inaugurated with a shout. It will be climaxed with a shout, for the Lord, Himself, will descend with a shout, and the saints shall be raised and His people raptured. They will hear His voice and all who hear shall live. Then shall He come with ten thousands of His saints. 'The Lord shall roar from on high, and utter His voice from His holy habitation; He shall give a shout, as they that tread the grapes, against all the inhabitants of the earth.'[2] The headstone shall be brought forth with shoutings, and converted Israel cry, 'Grace, grace unto it'.[3] Meanwhile today men hear His still small voice. At first a whisper, then like thunder, his voice drowns out our Saul-like bluster. The voice that arrests at the gate, is the voice that charms us in the closet. Soon Ruth would be saying 'Let me see thy countenance, let me hear thy voice, for sweet is thy voice and thy countenance is comely. But she would say this only as learned from her loved one. For these, first of all, are the words of the bridegroom; but when whispered back, are his song of all songs.[4]

Thus Boaz, like the one he portends, ushers in his redeeming work with a shout. All eyes turn upon him. They have never heard him lift his voice. But then this is not an instruction to workers. This is a transaction. The unnamed kinsman sits and listens. Boaz rehearses the need of the helpless. What will he do?

'Naomi,' he says, 'that is come again out of the country of Moab, selleth a parcel of land,[5] which was our brother Elimelech's: and I thought to advertise thee, saying, Buy it before the inhabitants and before the elders of my people . . .' The thought of 'the uncovering' continues. Ruth uncovered Boaz's feet in the night. Her face was uncovered in the dawn, and now Boaz uncovers the ear of his kinsman, for that is the literal meaning of the word 'advertise'. When God moves forward in grace, there is always an unveiling and uncovering of things. He becomes disclosed to us and we made known to Him. His heart and ours are manifest. There is conviction and conversion. We see the Saviour and our sin. The world looks on, and sees God's love uncovered too. What Boaz does, is not done in a corner. It is done before all. Transgression was often exposed at the gate, but how much better the unveiling of grace, than the derobing of judgment. 'Moab shall die with shouting,' says Amos.[6] Ruth was ready for the triumph of Boaz. His shout at the gate meant death to her ancestry. It opened a way to her new generation, and that was her gladness. She would never suffer now the condemnation of her people. The Moabite in her was judged already. She would be a bride of a prince in Israel. If we will accept all that Christ has done for us in the gate, and acknowledge His total claim as bought with a price, then our old man is indeed crucified with Him. It is judged in His cross. We are linked for ever in life with the Prince of Peace. We are the bearers of His Name. Jesus shouted when He died for me. And should not I shout as dying with Him. O 'let them shout for joy and be glad, that favour *My* righteousness.'[7]

'Now,' says Boaz to his kinsman, 'if thou wilt redeem it, redeem it: but if thou wilt not redeem it, then tell me, that I may know: for there is none to redeem it beside thee: and I am after thee.'

And he said, 'I will redeem it.'

Then said Boaz, 'What day thou buyest the field of the hand of Naomi, thou must buy it also of Ruth, the Moabitess, the wife of the dead, to raise up the name of the dead upon his inherit-ance.'[8]

And the kinsman said, 'I cannot redeem it for myself, lest I mar mine own inheritance: redeem thou my right to thyself; for I cannot redeem it.'

There are three things that come to light in this most intri-guing conversation. They are, the right, the readiness and the resources to redeem. The Law of redemption enunciated in Leviticus twenty-five had to do with the redemption of both property and persons. God is concerned not simply with what a person has but who a person is. Both Ruth and the field must come under the redemption. Redemption is a total concept and affects both what we have and what we are. As to our persons, redemption first takes up the spirit, is then expressed in the soul and finally lays hold on the body and lifts it to resurrection glory. As to our possessions it lays claim on our substance, our time, our talents, our opportunities and spiritual gifts. There is nothing we have, be it temporal, eternal, natural or spiritual that we did not receive. We have no rights. By creation, provision, protection and redemption, all that we have and all that we are, is totally the Redeemer's. What we must remember is, that redemption and its acceptance involves, of necessity, an admittance of impotence on the part of its object. It implies a total inadequacy and utter bankruptcy in those it lifts. The unredeemed always maintain they are 'their own'. The first thing the redeemed must learn is that he is 'not his own'. This lesson is made easier when viewed from the positive angle, for whilst my person and property become my Redeemer's, the wonderful thing is that His Person and His property become mine; mine, of course, not as independent of Him but as one with Him. It means that through the redemption that is in Christ Jesus, all that I am and have, becomes His, and all that He is and has, becomes mine. We are joint-heirs with Christ. We are joined unto the Lord. We are one spirit, just as a man joined to his wife is one flesh. We have all things in common. Once redeemed, Ruth's heart would anticipate the words of the Shunamite concerning Solomon, her great, great grandson. 'I am my beloved's and my beloved is mine.' She and hers had been purchased; He, and all His, bestowed.

At the gate of Bethlehem, we see the two kinsmen set in contrast to each other. There is the first man, the nearest relation after the flesh; and there is the second man, Boaz, who steps in, where the first man fails. Representatively these two men can speak to us of the first Adam, and the Last Adam whom the first prefigured. We sometimes think of Adam and Eve as falling together, but this was not so. There are four distinct phases in the 'Adam and Eve' relationship. First of all, there was the period when Adam was without Eve, and unfallen. Secondly, there was the period when Adam and Eve were together and they were both unfallen. Thirdly, there was the period when Adam was still unfallen, though Eve had fallen. Finally, there was the period when Adam fell, and he and Eve were then both together in their shame. The most crucial period for Adam was, of course, the third one. It is perhaps not unreasonable to suppose, that at that fearful juncture, when Eve was cut off from communion with God and in league with the adversary, Adam, being still unfallen, might have pondered, with grief, her awful fate. One would have thought that he would have enquired of God concerning her, considering she was condemned to die. Adam, still unstained, was as perfect as in the day first created. Whilst incapable of being the true mediator, being only human and not divine, he could have at least morally, and in love for the woman, offered to die in her place. He might have cried like Moses, 'Let my name be blotted out of thy book, if only she might live.' But Adam, even if able, was not willing; and Moses, though willing, was certainly not able.

Adam is our first kinsman, but he never raised the thought of redemption. He chose rather to go with the woman in the way she had taken. He fell to where she was. He never thought of a way to lift her to where he stood. Somehow he viewed his prospects blighted without her, so out he went from God. How many since, have confirmed that downward road in their own experience. They have dared to say, in effect, better a woman without God, than to walk with God without a woman. The natural man can never produce the spiritual. The first kinsman, Adam could never redeem. He could never provide a ransom for himself, much less for us his posterity. The words are true, 'I cannot redeem'. Adam, originally, might in one sense have had the right to redeem, but he had not the readiness. The man in our story had the right, and initially, the readiness, but when it came to it, he lacked the resources. Only the second man, the Lord from heaven, that pillar of strength, that Boaz of God upholding all things for us and for heaven, combined these three great requirements. He was willing to seal the entire trans-action with His own life's blood.

Thinking again of the man in our story, he phrases his

contention thus: I cannot redeem it for myself, lest I mar mine own inheritance. It may have been, of course, that he was currently married. It may have been that he had children through an earlier marriage to whom he wished to leave all he had. Maybe he felt his good name would be impaired by marrying a Moabitess and his posterity would blame him for confusing the blood of Israel with that of an alien. Maybe there were other reasons too. The contention, though, does raise the matter of resources. If he paid out Naomi and Ruth for the field it may be he would have to sell some of his own estate to raise the funds. This could cause an outcry in his own more immediate family circle. They would view themselves as impoverished beneficiaries under the final settlement of the inheritance. The purchased field would never be theirs. It would pertain to the offspring of the new wife coming in. To take Ruth to himself, a woman in whom he had shown no interest, and at the same time completely confound his own family affairs, was really quite beyond him. It seems he had neither the spiritual character, nor the material resources to handle her case. Like the boasting of our own Adamic flesh, which starts away with such self-confidence, he proved quite hopeless in the end. Turning therefore to Boaz, he removes his shoe as the custom required and says to him, 'Buy it for yourself!' He passes as he came, a kinsman, but nameless on the page. He loved his life and lost his chances; and finds no comeback.

Boaz stands out now as the one who meets all the qualifications of the redeemer. Having the right, he shows himself ready. His ample resources are mustered for action. To use a modern expression, he 'has what it takes'. He is the 'gaal' the one with whom now lie the prerogatives of redemption. It is an interesting word in Scripture and is expressed diversely, as required by the context, for kinsman, avenger and deliverer. These three characteristics are all brought out in the Lord Jesus Christ, the second Man, who did what Adam failed to do. The writer to the Hebrews puts it thus:

'Forasmuch then as the children are partakers of flesh and blood, He also Himself likewise took part of the same:

This makes Him our *kinsman*.

'that through death He might destroy him that had the power of death, that is, the devil;

This shows Him the *avenger*.

'And deliver them who through fear of death were all their lifetime subject to bondage.'⁹

This proclaims Him the *deliverer*.

Whilst Boaz is sitting in the gate, Ruth, it seems, is sitting still at home. This was Naomi's injunction. Normally, when a legally qualified kinsman refused, for personal reasons, to do the kinsman's part, the outraged widow would be present to pull off his shoe and spit in his face, saying as she did so, 'Thus shall it be done unto that man that will not build up his brother's house.' The stubborn refusal in such a case was a matter of social shame and the man with his household was called, 'The house of him that hath his shoe loosed.'¹⁰ In the situation at the gate, however, the man took off his own shoe, and Ruth was not present to spit in his face. It would appear that she had already tasted so deeply of God's grace that she did not exact the letter of the Law. In view of Ruth's preference for Boaz, it was hardly needful to add humiliation to defeat. The man, no doubt, was sufficiently humbled by the debacle of his own inability for his failure to be emphasised. It teaches us to find out the facts, ere we voice our intentions.

When we think of the selfless devotion of our Lord Jesus Christ and of his utter readiness to effect our redemption, the more amazing it becomes to see how he was treated, both by Jew and Gentile. He was treated as if He had no right to redeem; as if He were unwilling to redeem; and as if He had no powers to redeem. His heel was made bare and the serpent bruised it. The children of men—they spat in His face. Shoeless and spittle-smeared, Christ went to Calvary. He looked like the first Adam who failed to redeem; but He is The Last, who saves us for ever.

But why should the man in the story take off his shoe? someone will ask. The answer is more apparent than at first appears. When Joshua led the hosts of Israel in the conquest of Canaan, he did so with a certain promise rising in his heart.

God had said, 'Arise, go over this Jordan, thou and all this people, unto the land which I do give them, even to the children of Israel. Every place that the sole of your foot shall tread upon, that have I given unto you, as I said unto Moses.' The shoe, symbolical of a foot placed on the ground, indicates the right of possession.[11] To take it off before witnesses in a land transaction such as this, was to give notice that all one's rights to tread on that property were now relinquished. To have it pulled off by the other party asserted the matter, of course, even more forcibly. It meant surely that one was publicly deprived of the rights concerned. But in either case the meaning is clear. It is further illustrated in two of the Psalms where the Lord says, 'Moab is my washpot; over Edom will I cast out my shoe'.[12]

Jesus came first in sandals, and John the Baptist felt unworthy to unloose them. What then shall men do when He comes, His feet like burnished brass and bright with flame? The feet that climbed Mount Calvary, and sheathed the cruel nails, shall stand at last on Olivet. Then shall The Meek inherit the earth and the Almighty's word find its fulfilment. 'Sit Thou on my right hand,' He says, 'until I make Thine enemies, Thy footstool.' When His feet are uncovered in that day, the universe will be beneath them. The feet of the Redeemer are beautiful now. They bring good tidings. At the last they shall tread the winepress of the wrath of God. He is our Kinsman and Deliverer, but He is our Avenger too.

NOTES

1. Lamentations 3:8
2. Jeremiah 25:30
3. Zechariah 4:7
4. Canticles 2:10; 1:1, 2
5. It has been inferred that this expression concerns a kind of feudal right of tillage in part of a common field, but it is difficult to reconcile this with the more absolute concepts of possession and inheritance prevalent in Israel in the time of Boaz and Ruth.
6. Amos 2:2
7. Psalm 35:27
8. See Numbers 27:6–11 regarding the law of inheritance in Israel.
9. Hebrews 2:14, 15
10. Deuteronomy 25:5–10
11. See also Deuteronomy 1:36 'to Caleb will I give the land that he hath trodden upon . . .'
12. Psalms 60 and 108

Twenty-two

The Declaration

> '*He that hath the bride is the bridegroom.*'
> '*He that hath received His testimony hath set to his seal that God is true.*'
>
> John 3: 29, 33

I n the limited community of Bethlehem, the news of events at the gate filtered quickly back through the stalls and the honeycombed streets. People rapidly assembled until it looked as if half the town were there. Although Ruth seems to have been absent from the preliminary discussion as to who her redeemer would be, there is little doubt that she and Naomi were now summoned to appear with Boaz before the elders at the gate. The original title of the land, carefully preserved by Naomi, was asked for and produced. The silver was weighed and handed over, and then the declaration of intent was publicly avowed by Boaz. The esteem and affection in which Ruth had come to be held, coupled with the honour and standing of Boaz in the locality, made the transaction something of a sensation. The people waited patiently as all the business was effected. The seals were affixed and the witnesses given. Then at last there was a stir as Boaz rose to speak before the company of those present. With a voice full of dignity, yet charged with emotion, he made his awaited speech. His words were more than sentiment. They were a declaration recorded, not only on earth, but in the very annals of heaven.

'Ye are witnesses this day,' he began, turning first to the elders and then to the people. As his eyes swept the onlookers, they felt themselves drawn in to the solemnity of this vital transaction. They were no mere observers but participators, whose testimony must count. 'Ye are witnesses', he said, 'that I have bought all that was Elimelech's, and all that was Chilion's and Mahlon's, of the hand of Naomi. Moreover Ruth the Moabitess, the wife of Mahlon, have I purchased to be my wife, to raise up the name of the dead upon his inheritance, that the name of the dead be not cut off from among his brethren, and from the gate of his place: ye are witnesses this day.'

So the deed is done. It is all-inclusive and so far-reaching. The declaration is made. His loved one has been claimed; and the dead names live. 'I have bought all . . .' It is the grand finale, the consummation of a purpose of grace, pursued according to Law, and now confirmed and upheld by Law. Ruth holds her position before God and before men in Israel, through a grace that reigns on the ground of righteousness. She takes her place in the genealogy of Christ. Her name is engraved in His Book in heaven, and written for ever in the Book below. She becomes one of the Gentile brides in the history of Israel, whose name extols for ever the wider mercies of our God. We think of Joseph and his Asenath, depicting the Church with Christ in glory. We think of Moses and Zipporah, depicting the Church with Christ in rejection. We think again of Salmon and Rahab. They tell of that *out of* which grace brought us; and here, we have Boaz and Ruth, who speak of that *into* which grace has brought us. Ruth thus takes her place along side the three other women mentioned in the ancestry of Christ.[1] The darkness from which they were lifted accentuates for us the light of God that shone upon them. There was Tamar, who pretended to be a harlot. Rahab, who was a harlot. Bathsheba, who played the harlot; and Ruth delivered from a nation of harlots.[2]

Yet God in his grace made each of these a bride and a wife, whose offspring stand in the lineage of His Son. It is His way, and magnifies His Name. Down all the years He does this very thing. From Gentile nations guilty of the worst iniquity, He brings a people to His love and favour. From the Jewish race, with all their failings, he draws a blood-bought ransomed throng. There is neither Jew nor Gentile. He makes us one new man in Christ. Out from our varied walks of life, from our varied religions and attendant cultures, from every tongue and people and nation, we are coming to Jesus. What we were and what we thought; the things we did, and said and planned; all are erased. There is neither black nor white, male or female, bond or free. We are stepping out of Adam into Christ. Through His cross all that we were in Adam is annulled. We are loosed from our sins in His own blood. We are not our own. We are constituted one living Body, a holy bride 'without spot, or wrinkle, or any such thing'. His future has become our own.

The road from the outback of Moab to the intimacy of Boaz has reached its wondrous conclusion. The darkness is past and the true light now shines. The love of God has conquered, and is filling both their hearts. It is a story to thrill the redeemed in whatever age they live; a love-song in harvest, that leads us to glory.

Paul Gerhardt knew the melody. His lines live on:

> *O the blessed joy of meeting,*
> *All the desert past!*
> *O the wondrous words of greeting*
> *He shall speak at last.*
> *He and I together entering*
> *Those bright courts above;*
> *He and I together sharing*
> *All the Father's love.*
>
> *He, who in the hour of sorrow*
> *Bore the curse alone;*
> *I, who through the lonely desert*
> *Trod where He had gone.*
> *He and I in that bright glory*
> *One deep joy shall share;*
> *Mine to be for ever with Him,*
> *His, that I am there.*

NOTES

1. Matt. 1 : 3, 5, 6
2. Numbers 25 : 1

Twenty-three

The Audience Response

> '*The woman saith unto Him, I know that Messias cometh, which is called Christ: when he is come, He will tell us all things. Jesus saith unto her, I that speak unto thee am He.*'
> '*And upon this came His disciples, and marvelled that He talked with the woman: yet no man said, What seekest Thou? or, Why talkest Thou with her?*'
>
> John 4: 25, 26, 27

THE spontaneous answer of the assembled crowd, led by the elders, is most striking. 'Witnesses!' they shout. 'We are witnesses!' They represent the Law and the nation. This is the kind of acclaim Jesus Christ should have received, the first time He came; but when at last, as our heavenly Boaz, He stands with His Church before them, Israel will own Him then. Looking back we can say with Peter, 'to Him give all the prophets witness;' and with Paul, His righteousness is 'witnessed by the Law and the prophets.' In this regard, the Father bore witness of Him, and His works, too, declared Him. The apostles were ordained His witnesses and we who believe today, witness to Jesus as Lord to the ends of the earth. Yes, we are witnesses. This is our glad confession of the Redeemer who has bought us all, and holds us as His bride by right of purchase. His biggest witness in our story is, of course, in Ruth herself. Wherever she went, she would be a living memorial to what Boaz, in God's grace, had done for her.

After this the people and the elders voice their aspirations for the bride and bridegroom. Ruth is never called a Moabitess again, for all that was of Moab about her had died with the shouting. She is now referred to as 'the woman that is come in to thine house'. They no longer refer to her earlier background, but own her now in her new found place. She is 'the woman who has been brought in . . .' She has gleaned in the fields of Boaz; she has sat at his table in harvest; she has tasted his bread and drunk of his well. She has lain at his feet but now she is received into his house and finds rest in his love. What began at barley harvest has been climaxed in wheat harvest. What begins at the cross is realised at Pentecost. All leads to His house and our dwelling for ever. His Presence is our final abode. He wants us there. Shall not the heart of His loved one reply, 'One thing have I desired of the Lord, that will I seek after; that I may dwell in the house of the Lord all the days of my life, to behold the beauty of the Lord, and to inquire in His temple.'

Their prayer for Ruth is that she should be 'like Rachel and like Leah, which two did build the house of Israel.' Such hopes would be exceeded. Of the two daughters of Laban, Rachel was more loved by Jacob, though Leah was more fruitful. Together they laid the foundations of the house of Israel. The offspring of Ruth would find himself in the full flow of these purposes, and as for Ruth, she would be more loved than Rachel, for she was the only beloved of Boaz, her husband. She shared his affection with no other. She was his bride alone. And then also, she was more 'fruitful' than Leah. Leah bore but six sons, whereas Ruth in the birth of Obed is declared as being better than seven. Notice that Rachel is set before Leah. Rachel is first for she was first to be loved, and love originates. Leah is mentioned after her, for the thought of fruitfulness emerges only after love prevails. Ruth was first a Rachel to Boaz, loved with a love that would not change; a love so strong that it paid the price. Afterwards, Ruth was his Leah: the initial blessings of the field were realised now in the blessings of the womb. She bore him an heir. Boaz was a descendant of Leah, through her son Judah. God's sceptre was with him. As Rachel and Leah built the house of Israel, so Boaz and Ruth would build the house of the kings. Nationhood was one thing, but through Obed, God's royal line would be established. What destiny in days of anarchy! Elimelech's name now lived again. God reigned. This family and its history proved it yet.

The response goes on. 'And do thou worthily in Ephratah,

and be famous in Bethlehem.' True fame should be rooted in true worth. Cheap promotion may create an image, but only excellence, a name. The word 'worthily' is the Hebrew 'chayil' and implies to act with 'strength or might'. Although differently translated, the same word gives weight to the riches of Boaz in chapter two and the virtue of Ruth in chapter three. All their material and moral resources are now to be concentrated in their mutual future, to the praise and glory of God. Their worth in the community will establish their distinction. Ruth, who was barren in Moab, bears now in Israel. She is knit with Ephratah, 'the place of fertility'. She might have been voluptuous, like many of her sisters, but she remained virtuous, and God made her fruitful. Her life before Him gave her standing in Bethlehem. The fame that counts, rests not in a fan mail, but in God's favour. What is earth's lauding, if heaven should frown; or man's reward, if God rebuke. Our story began with a famine in Bethlehem but now comes the fame. The famine told of God's disfavour, but fame like this, of God's good pleasure. Men lauded our Lord, but what they said added nothing to Him. He was what He was, the Great I AM. First it was a whispered fame.[1] Then he became the talk of the town;[2] and finally the theme of a reasoned discussion.[3] But none of these things moved Him. It was the Father's pleasure that sustained him. There were many voices, but the voice of the Father was enough for Jesus. Neither places, nor persons made Jesus great. It was their life with Him that gave *them* meaning. This was the kind of fame which Boaz and his Ruth desired, a fame for ever in God's loving favour. True greatness here on earth rests wholly on that greatness grace bestows. The verdict of the Highest is the saint's concern. All else is vain.

Their final wish for the newlyweds is touching. 'Let thy house be like the house of Pharez, whom Tamar bore unto Judah, of the seed which the Lord shall give thee of this young woman.' Perhaps Ruth's youth should first be noted.

There appear to be three words for 'the young' in The Book of Ruth. Boaz uses two, when describing his young men. In the field he speaks of them in terms which mean they are 'growing persons'. In the night, however, when speaking to Ruth, he refers to them as 'unmarried persons'. The word used

for Ruth, simply means a young female person and does not
take cognisance of any past marital relationship. She is not
called a widow, or even a young widow. Everything for her is
new in Boaz. The old things of Mahlon have passed away. She
is no longer viewed as bereaved, or broken. She is a young
woman on the threshold of union with her redeemer-bride-
groom, and stands as if she had known no other. This kind of
'newness' only God can give. She had waited on the Lord and
He had renewed her strength. Now her youth was renewed like
the eagles. Youth tends to follow youth; but youth can rarely
mature youth. Ruth, the young, had followed Naomi the older.
Under her guidance, she had been led to Boaz. She followed not
after young men, whether poor or rich. In Boaz, she had come
to one who was mature and stable and of proven worth. She was
under his wing, a pinion that had weathered the storm.

We now come to the story of Tamar's relations with Judah,
her father-in-law. It is a sordid tale. The more one reads the
Bible, the more one realises that the divine emphasis on sex-
relations is not primarily on the pleasure derived but upon the
children born. Today's concepts are quite the reverse. The idea
of many is to extort as much sensation from the sex-act as
possible and to prevent the 'encumbrance' of children by
contraception or abortion. Consequently, there is as much
'prostitution' of sex in the married state, as there is outside of it.
There is a tendency to feel that once one is properly married,
then within the fabric of the relationship one can do what one
likes. After all what does it matter? The story of Tamar and her
marital affairs shows that it matters very much. God is present
in our privacy. The real force of the story in Genesis chapter
thirty-eight, is that through all the vagaries of the affairs there
described, God was bringing through the Messianic line. The
emotions, passions and delusions of the family of Judah, whilst
of concern to God and inviting judgment, were not in themselves, primary. The raising up of the seed of Judah, rather,
was paramount, for of that lineage was to come the Lion of the
tribe of Judah, Jesus Christ Himself. Any attempt to frustrate
that development was Satanic, and Onan died for it. After the
death of his wife, Judah, who had broken his word to His
daughter-in-law, is caught out by her disguise and she is found

with child, by him, much to his chagrin. Tamar is not exonerated in her method but she is in her intention. She was the only one in the whole family concerned about the continuity of the line, and she was a Gentile at that. Judah admits, 'She has been more righteous than I'. God gives Tamar conception and she bears twins, Zarah, her firstborn and Pharez, his brother. God is so meticulously concerned about all this that the minutest details of the births are given.

Now it might well be asked, why is all this mentioned in connection with Ruth. First of all, the genealogy at the end of The Book of Ruth shows that Boaz is a descendant of Pharez. And secondly, the story of Tamar provides the reader with a comparable incident in earlier days. The first kinsman in our story behaved rather like Judah did towards Tamar. He was dilatory in raising up seed for his next of kin. Had Boaz not stepped in, all would have been lost. As the Gentile, Tamar was honoured in bearing Pharez, so may Ruth, the people are saying, be honoured in bearing seed for Boaz. The Messianic line is very slender, although the single thread is strong. It is remarkable that both Tamar and Ruth, outsiders, introduced through grace, should be used to preserve it; and not only that, but should do so with such obvious intelligence. The utterance of the Bethlehemites was prophetic, not only in the fact that they spoke of the seed that the Lord would give, but in the Messianic import this word contained.[4] It was not just an expression of good wishes but a categorical statement that Ruth would bear a son of consequence. When Judah failed, Tamar acted. When the first kinsman failed, Boaz stepped in. It is not for nothing. God was going to have His way.

'Children are a heritage of the Lord: and the fruit of the womb is His reward.'[5] However irresponsible sex-relations may be, and God never condones irresponsibility, notwithstanding, no child enters upon life independent of the direct action of the Creator. Whatever the midwife or the physician may do, Paul asserts this fact when he describes his birth in his Galatian letter. He speaks of 'God, who separated me from my mother's womb'.[6] The act is His and not another's. From the day of our birth to the day of our death, God must be acknowledged as the author of our life. It is true of our first and natural birth; and it

is true of our new, and spiritual birth. It is God who gives
conception. It is God who grants regeneration. It is God who
brings to birth both the children of men and the children of
God. It is because we owe our life to God that we are ever
accountable to God. Obed when he came, therefore, was
recognised as a gift from God. He was the child the Lord had
promised and a child the Lord had given. Obed was not the
fortuitous outcome of a love affair between a local landlord and a
foreign girl from across the river. This was, in a very special
way, God's child of the moment. All God's interests lay in that
tiny babe at this point in history. Babies can be as important as
that, though we might not think so. God is the author of sex
and the governor of its functions. We may prostitute the seed
of the man and crucify the Seed of the woman but not without
consequence. If we do not let our Lord write our love-story,
we shall never glorify Him in it; and if we do not glorify Him
in that, it is doubtful if we shall ever glorify Him at all. As
Whitefield, the great evangelist prayed, when still in his
bachelor state, 'Lord keep me from having a wife, till I have
learned to have none'.

There is a scarlet thread in Scripture, a thread that divides.
Rahab, the mother of Boaz, was distinguished from her fellow-
citizens by the scarlet thread in the window. Zarah was distinguished from Pharez by the scarlet thread on his hand. It
marked him as the firstborn. Pharez for all his striving from the
womb, had never a natural claim on Judah his father. But God
passed by Zarah and chose Pharez the second. 'No flesh shall
glory in My Presence,' says the Lord. This is very strongly
established in the opening book of the Bible. God is laying
down the principle, once and for all. There were two brothers,
Cain and Abel. Cain was the elder but God's man was Abel,
and when he died, Seth took his place. There were two brothers,
Ishmael and Isaac. Ishmael was the elder, but God said, 'In
Isaac shall thy seed be called'. There were two brothers, Esau
and Jacob. Esau was the firstborn, but God loved Jacob and
gave him His covenant. There were two brothers, Reuben, the
firstborn of the first wife, and Joseph, the firstborn of the
second wife; but God chose Joseph, not Reuben, to bless the
world with bread. There were two brothers, Manasseh and

Ephraim, but Jacob crossed his hands, and with intention, blessed Ephraim, the younger. Zarah and Pharez were two brothers. The scarlet thread was the midwive's mark. This was not faith, like the faith of Rahab. Labelling our children does not make them God's children. Pharez proved to be chosen of God. God's man is not the first but the second. His blessing is not by human 'right' but by divine grace. He has mercy on whom He will have mercy. His heart is love, and it has its reasons, but being infinite, remains inscrutable. His salvation is not of blood(s), nor of the will of the flesh, nor of the will of man, but of God.⁷ His choice is not the elder, the symbol of our strength to beget, but the younger. He meets us not in 'the beginning of our strength' but when we are 'without strength'. We are not to boast in our generation but in His regeneration. There is no acceptance in our flesh, acceptance can only be in The Beloved. Boaz and Ruth stood in the glorious purpose of the God of Pharez and they walked on together towards the end of that road.

The fellow-labourer of the fields is joined to a fellow-kinsman. She becomes a fellow-citizen of the commonwealth of faith and now a fellow-heir of the grace of life.⁸ Introduced as a woman of Moab (1:4), she is finally seen as the bride of God's man and the hope of Israel. 'So Boaz took Ruth,' the narrative concludes, 'and she became his wife; and when he went in to her, the Lord gave conception, and she bare a son.' Note the moral order. The physical union *follows* the social and legal recognition of their new relationship. It does not precede it. The Bible never gives sanction at any time to pre-marital intercourse. God made one man. Then he formed one woman and she was taken *from* man that she might be *for* man. Eve was for Adam, and Adam then for Eve. They were never for anybody else. It was the divine intention from the beginning that one man should have one wife, and that one particular woman should be identified with one particular man. That ideal was never rescinded, whatever historical exceptions or Mosaic regulative injunctions intervened. When Christ was questioned on these matters, he went right back to the beginning and re-asserted God's original concept of union. The apostolic teachers expounded and endorsed this principle. Paul by the

Spirit, takes up the union of a man and his wife as illustrative of the union of Christ and His Church. The symbol is to be characterised by that which is permanent and pure, for it represents a spiritual relationship, both eternal and unsullied. The love of a man to his wife, therefore, must exhibit the selfless love of Christ for His own. If the symbol is to portray the substance, the principles governing the ultimate reality must be consistently displayed in the symbol. No one, in New Testament times, was tolerated in Church leadership, who would not uphold this standard before the pagan world.[9] The Church was adamant. To weaken on this point today, is to deny the moral foundations of the Church's abiding relationship to Jesus Christ her Lord. Marriage pertains to humanity, but is divine in origin. It is not, therefore, a subject for human innovation, but is to be subject rather, to God's regulation. The division of the sexes is established in creation. The blurring of the sex distinction in fashion, coiffure, role and function does despite, therefore, to the image of God in man, which the woman helps to define. The proper recognition of God is linked then with the proper distinction of the male and female. Without this there can also be no proper union, and with no proper union, no witness in marriage to the ideal relationship between God and His creature. In the light of this, sex perversion and fornication are akin to blasphemy.

Note again, it was the Lord who gave conception. With all the scientific advance of our times and its sometimes unwarranted intrusion into the processes of procreation, people still have the children they do not want and fail to have the children they desire. We do not need to read books about sex, especially if it is sex for sinners. If we read the Bible and our hearts are willing, we shall learn about God's sex for saints.

NOTES

1. Luke 4 : 14, 15
2. Luke 4 : 37
3. Luke 5 : 15
   Luke uses three different Greek words for 'fame' in these passages.
4. It is perhaps significant that the word here is singular, not 'seeds' but 'seed'. It reminds us of the importance attached to this mode of expression

in Galatians 3 : 16. 'He saith not, And to seeds, as of many; but as of one, And to thy seed, which is Christ.'
5. Psalm 127 : 3
6. Galatians 1 : 15
7. See John 1 : 12, 13
8. There are probably no better words in the whole of the New Testament to sum up Ruth's experience and that of the present day redeemed, than are found in Ephesians 2 : 11–19; especially the passage which reads: 'at that time ye were . . . aliens from the commonwealth of Israel, and strangers from the covenants of promise, having no hope, and without God in the world: But now . . . ye who sometimes were afar off are made nigh . . . ye are no more strangers and foreigners but fellow-citizens with the saints and of the household of God'.
9. I Timothy 3 : 2

Twenty-four

A Son for Naomi

'The Lord blessed the latter end . . . more than (the) beginning.'

Job 42: 12

'Despise not thou the chastening of the Lord, nor faint when thou art rebuked of Him . . . afterward it yieldeth the peaceable fruit of righteousness unto them which are exercised thereby.'

Hebrews 12: 5–11

I T was the barley harvest once again, when the baby was born. But all the rolling fields of grain could not compare, for Boaz, with the fruit of the womb. There had never been a harvest quite like this. The years of loneliness receded. Ruth had travailed, but so had he. There had always been children in Bethlehem but this was his child, the heir of all things. The first day they took their little son out in the open, they laid him in Naomi's arms, as she sat in the old paved courtyard. Beyond the gate stretched a vista of blue, where the hills grew wistful in a haze of heat. In the shimmering east lay the land of her memories, which had silvered her hair and changed her to Mara. Not far away was the field where they toiled. Then it was a dust bowl but now redeemed, it rippled in the sun, alive with corn. She had sown with weeping. Now they were bringing in the sheaves. She was Naomi again and there was no more Moab. She would never go back, though they were buried there. Her home was in Bethlehem in the land of her fathers. Here she tasted His bread and drank in His Presence. This was the new time. The old times were fading. In the peace of the child, He was wiping her tears. The breeze stirred faintly in the gnarled old mulberry. Its leaves clapped joyfully and then kept silence. Two dark brown eyes, like resin in the snow, looked upward to eternity. Two little eyelids closed. She felt the tiny fingers clasp her breast. She never nursed a child in Moab. Her emptiness was filled . . .

The local women called him Obed,[1] a princely child, yet born to serve. No doubt, Ruth's industry inspired his name. Along the hilltop path, the peasant girls filed by. They were the reapers. Some carried water homeward, or provisions from the town. Last year Ruth gleaned amongst them, yet they rejoiced for her and Boaz. Some halted briefly for a greeting, then glimpsed the young one in the old one's arms. Glad for a respite in their arduous climb, they placed their loads on the rough stone wall, then tiptoed softly to the babe.

'A son for Naomi,' they whispered. She shared their wonder. 'He is the restorer of your life,' they chanted.[2] The words, so fitly chosen, expressed the very mind of God. In Obed, death's dark tide was turning. Now the gates of life were opening. Isaiah later used the word. 'And they that be of thee', he wrote, 'shall build the old wasteplaces: thou shalt raise up the foundations of many generations; and thou shalt be called the repairer of the breach, the restorer of paths to dwell in.' Into such a destiny this little child was growing.

'He is your nourisher in time of age.'[3] This was their song. God's loving kindness filled her heart. She was not left without a kinsman.[4]

The sun went down and Ruth emerged. She took the child and held it to her. She paused a moment on the threshold, her eyes like stars, her face serene. A wisp of mist like comet's hair swept upward through the dispersed light. A shaft of gold lit up the babe and Ruth grew radiant. She walked with Naomi through the archway. The shadows in the valleys deepened. Time seemed no more . . .

But O the glimpse of final splendour; the promise of another day. For in that moment of the sunset, Ephratah's fields were flushed with glory, and there beyond the glow and wonder, I heard the song of other voices, an angel host in Bethlehem's sky. I thought the shepherds in the hills must hear it; and all the world must surely echo it, this song of love to earth descending.

This song of The Child.

NOTES

1. 'Obed' means 'to serve'.
2. 'Restorer' means 'one who causes to turn back'.
3. 'Nourisher' means 'one who provides'.
4. This time, of course, meaning not Boaz but the child.

Bibliography

The American Journal of Semitic Languages and Literature
vol. lviii, no. 4, October 1941 article by John Garstang

BROWN, ROBERT *Gleanings from the Book of Ruth* S. W. Part-
ridge & Co., London

COATES, C. A., *Outline of the Book of Ruth and The Epistle of
James* London

COX, SAMUEL *The Book of Ruth*

EDERSHEIM, ALFRED 'Israel in Canaan' *Joshua and the Judges*

GARSTANG, JOHN and GARSTANG, J. R. E., *The Story of Jericho*
Marshall, Morgan & Scott, London 1948

KELLER, WERNER (translated from the German by William
Neil) *The Bible as History* Hodder & Stoughton, London
1956

KELLY, W., *Lectures on Joshua to II Samuel* London

MAURO, PHILIP *Ruth the Satisfied Stranger*

MOORHOUSE, HENRY *Ruth, the Moabitess and other Bible Readings*
Pickering & Inglis, London

MORRIS, LEON 'Ruth, an Introduction and Commentary' from
Judges and Ruth *The Tyndale Old Testament Commentaries*
London 1968

MORTON, H. V., *In the Steps of the Master* London 1953

THATCHER, G. W., 'Judges and Ruth' *The Century Bible*
Caxton Publishing Co., London 1904

VAN RYN, AUGUST 'Boaz and Ruth' *Redemption, Rest, Riches*
The Walterick Printing Co., Kansas City

WATSON, ROBERT A., 'Judges and Ruth' *The Expositor's Bible*